Silvia Gastaldi - Claire Musat

M000276293

PEOPLE OF THE BIBLE

LIFE AND CUSTOMS

ST. ANTHONY MESSENGER PRESS
Cincinnati, Ohio

Introduction

Close your eyes. Think back to last Christmas. Where were you? What were you doing?

Now try to think back even further in time. Make an extra effort, think back a long way, long before you were born. Imagine how your grandparents lived when they were your age. Their lives were certainly very different from yours. Think what the world would be like without computers, television, even telephones!

In this book we're going back even further, back and back in time until we get to the age of Jesus. Even then we won't be stopping. Before Jesus there was a world which we learn about from the pages of the Old Testament. If we think back that far, we may find ourselves following a caravan of camels carrying their loads across the desert under a burning sun. We may see large families all living together each in their own tents. How did they get on? Why did some of them decide to settle down? And what was life like when they did?

This is the sort of question to which you will find some answers in this book. It will show you all kinds of fascinating details of everyday life in town and village, among the rich and the poor, in palaces and temples and in the countryside, as it was lived from the time of Abraham to the time of Jesus.

Open the book, and you will find yourself on a journey through time. In it you will find fifty double-page spreads, fifty picture windows, each opening up on a different theme. Through them you will see many different views of a distant world which will slowly become more familiar to you.

Look, for instance, at the spread about education in biblical times. Were there books and blackboards? How did people learn? Or look at a spread about living conditions. There was no running water and people slept with animals. A few pages later there is a picture of a city gate: go through it and you will find narrow winding streets with all kinds of activities. Or you may want to go into the city of Jerusalem, into the heart of the temple. Or have a bird's-eye view of the land of Palestine.

The people of the Bible lived in a very different world from ours. But we have one very important thing in common with them. Like them, we have come to believe in God. So this book will also tell us something about our own past.

CONTENTS

PLACES, FACTS AND IDEAS

EVERYDAY LIFE

Panel 1: "YOU'RE TOO SEDENTARY, ALWAYS IN FRONT OF THE TV"

Panel 2: "LOOK AT ME, I'M SLIM ..."

Panel 3: "... DYNAMIC, AGILE, NOMADIC, LIKE THE ISRAELITES" ?!?

Panel 4: "NOMADIC, SEDENTARY? I DON'T KNOW WHAT THE ISRAELITES SAW IN IT!"

SANDRO '92

NOMADIC AND SEDENTARY

MANY PEOPLE IN THE BIBLE DIDN'T LIVE IN HOUSES BUT IN ...

TENTS

TRIBES OF SHEPHERDS, LIKE ABRAHAM'S, OFTEN MOVED AROUND IN SEARCH OF PASTURES. AT THE SAME TIME THEY TRIED TO KEEP CLOSE TO CULTIVATED LAND. THERE THEY MADE MORE STABLE CAMPS WHERE THEY KEPT CATTLE. THE SHEEP AND GOATS FOLLOWED THE SHEPHERDS, WHO WERE CONSTANTLY ON THE MOVE.

GOATSKINS OR FABRIC MADE FROM DARK GOATS' HAIR

THE INSIDE OF THE TENT IS RESERVED FOR WOMEN. ONLY THE HUSBAND MAY ENTER

FOOD AND COOKING UTENSILS ARE KEPT OUTSIDE NEAR THE TENT-PEGS

OPENING WHERE VISITORS WERE WELCOMED

SKIN AND JAR FOR WATER

COUNTERBALANCE WELL

MATS WERE PUT DOWN AS A FLOOR

WATER SUPPLIES WERE VITAL FOR FLOCKS AND SHEPHERDS. WATER WAS SO IMPORTANT THAT DISPUTES SOMETIMES FLARED UP BETWEEN DIFFERENT GROUPS WANTING TO USE THE SAME WELL.

THE SHEPHERD

THE FLOCK PROVIDES MEAT, WOOL, LEATHER AND MILK (FROM WHICH BUTTER, CHEESE AND YOGURT ARE MADE).

SHEARING TAKES PLACE IN SPRING, FOLLOWED BY A FEAST WHICH LASTS SEVERAL DAYS.

DURING THE DAY THE SHEEP AND GOATS GRAZE FREELY ROUND THE WATERING PLACES.
AT NIGHT THE FLOCK IS GATHERED INTO A FIELD SURROUNDED WITH A STONE WALL.

THE FARMER

FARMERS LIVE IN THE VILLAGES NEAR THEIR FIELDS. THE WHOLE FAMILY WORKS ON THE LAND. THE WORK IS VERY HARD, SINCE THERE ARE MANY STONES AND THORNS. THAT IS WHY THE SOWING COMES FIRST (CORN, BARLEY, MILLET), THEN THE PLOUGHING.

A SHEPHERD'S EQUIPMENT

CATAPULT AND STAFF FOR DEFENDING THE FLOCK AGAINST LIONS, BEARS, HYENAS AND JACKALS

LEATHER BAG FOR FOOD

CROOK (ABOUT SIX FEET LONG) FOR COUNTING SHEEP AND AS A WALKING STICK ON STEEP GROUND

THE FARMER'S EQUIPMENT

BASKET OR BAG FOR SOWING

YOKE FOR OXEN

PLOUGH

IRON POINT

SICKLE FOR REAPING

MATTOCK FOR CLEARING THE GROUND OF WEEDS

BY HAND

FLAIL

OR

THE GRAIN IS THRESHED WITH A STICK

WITH A SLEDGE PULLED BY ANIMALS WHICH GRINDS THE GRAIN

WINNOWING FAN

THE GRAIN AND THE CHAFF ARE FORKED AND THROWN IN THE AIR. THE CHAFF, WHICH IS LIGHTER, IS CARRIED AWAY BY THE WIND; THE HEAVIER GRAIN FALLS TO THE GROUND.

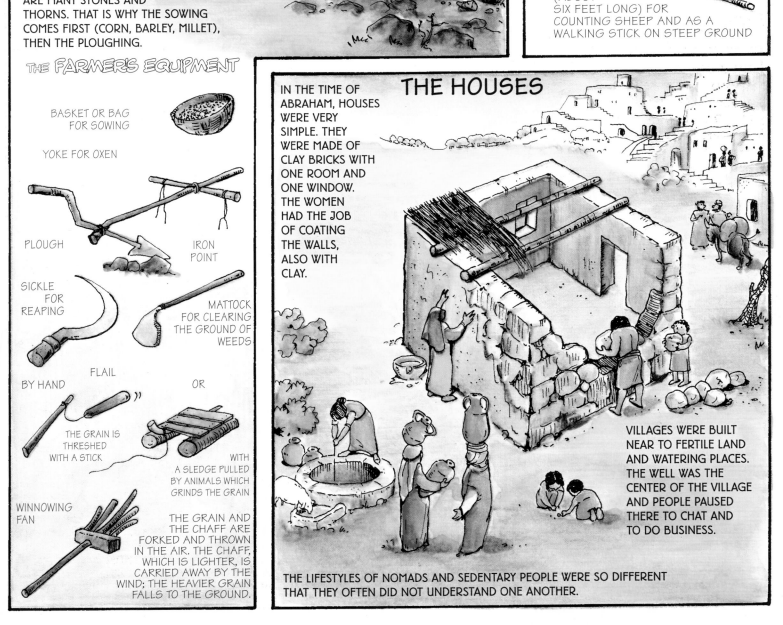

THE HOUSES

IN THE TIME OF ABRAHAM, HOUSES WERE VERY SIMPLE. THEY WERE MADE OF CLAY BRICKS WITH ONE ROOM AND ONE WINDOW. THE WOMEN HAD THE JOB OF COATING THE WALLS, ALSO WITH CLAY.

VILLAGES WERE BUILT NEAR TO FERTILE LAND AND WATERING PLACES. THE WELL WAS THE CENTER OF THE VILLAGE AND PEOPLE PAUSED THERE TO CHAT AND TO DO BUSINESS.

THE LIFESTYLES OF NOMADS AND SEDENTARY PEOPLE WERE SO DIFFERENT THAT THEY OFTEN DID NOT UNDERSTAND ONE ANOTHER.

FOR LUNCH, KING SOLOMON HAD VENISON

... WILD GOAT, ANTELOPE, HARE

... ALL KINDS OF GAME AND EXOTIC FRUIT...

NOT SOUP LIKE ME !!

LOOKING FOR FOOD

HUNTING

NUMEROUS ANCIENT SCULPTURES AND PAINTINGS SHOW US THAT HUNTING WAS A SPORTING ACTIVITY VERY POPULAR WITH THE NOBILITY AND KINGS OF EGYPT AND MESOPOTAMIA.

THE OLD TESTAMENT TELLS US THAT ORDINARY PEOPLE WHO CAME TO CANAAN HAD TO HUNT. THE MOUNTAINS AND THE JORDAN VALLEY WERE COVERED WITH DENSE VEGETATION IN WHICH THERE WERE MANY WILD ANIMALS. THESE WERE A DANGER TO HUMAN BEINGS AND FLOCKS.

Genesis 25.27

Judges 14.5-6

I Samuel 17.34-36

THERE WAS PLENTY OF GAME ON SOLOMON'S TABLE: VENISON, WILD GOAT, ANTELOPE AND OTHER SPECIES. THEY WERE HUNTED BY BOW AND ARROW OR CAUGHT IN TRAPS.

GNAM GNAM

IN **NEW TESTAMENT** TIMES HUNTING WAS DIFFICULT AND LESS COMMON. AGRICULTURE WAS EVERYWHERE AND EACH PARCEL OF LAND WAS CULTIVATED. HILLSIDES WERE TERRACED, AND EVERY DROP OF WATER WAS COLLECTED IN CISTERNS.

HONEY

TERRA COTTA TUBES STOPPED UP AT THE END WITH SOFT CLAY

HOLES BY WHICH THE BEES GO IN AND OUT

EARTH TO KEEP OFF THE SUN

IRON HOOK FOR GETTING OUT THE HONEYCOMBS

HONEY WAS USED AS AN INGREDIENT IN MANY CAKES AND BISCUITS. IT WAS PARTICULARLY GOOD FOR GROWING CHILDREN AND AS A MEDICINE.

HONEY WAS A VERY IMPORTANT FOOD AS SUGAR WAS UNKNOWN. WILD HONEY WAS USED. IT WAS PRODUCED BY BEES IN CLEFTS IN THE ROCK AND IN THE TRUNKS OF TREES.

ONLY LATER, IN NEW TESTAMENT TIMES, DO NUMEROUS TEXTS TALK ABOUT BEE-KEEPING AND EXTRACTING THE HONEY.

FISHING

IN OLD TESTAMENT TIMES THE ISRAELITES WERE NOT VERY FAMILIAR WITH SAILING. FISHING DEVELOPED ONLY IN NEW TESTAMENT TIMES AND ONLY ON THE SEA OF GALILEE. THIS WAS FULL OF FISH. THE BEST TIME FOR FISHING WAS BETWEEN DECEMBER AND APRIL.
NIGHTS WITH A FULL MOON WERE PARTICULARLY GOOD FOR FISHING.

HOW DID THEY FISH?

WITH A DRAGNET

WITH A CASTING NET
(IN DEEPER WATER)

ALSO WITH HOOK AND LINE, MORE RARELY WITH A HARPOON

SEA OF GALILEE (OR LAKE TIBERIAS OR GENNESARET)

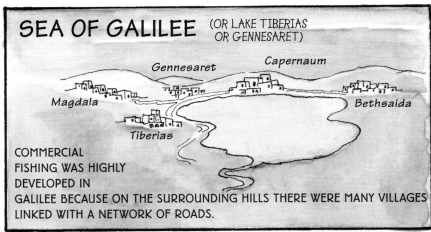

Gennesaret

Capernaum

Magdala

Bethsaida

Tiberias

COMMERCIAL FISHING WAS HIGHLY DEVELOPED IN GALILEE BECAUSE ON THE SURROUNDING HILLS THERE WERE MANY VILLAGES LINKED WITH A NETWORK OF ROADS.

THE FISH

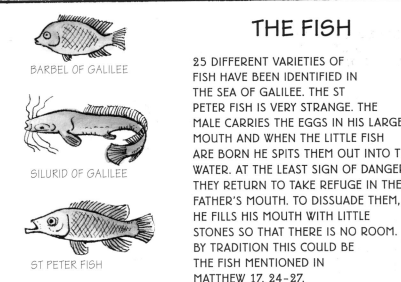

BARBEL OF GALILEE

SILURID OF GALILEE

ST PETER FISH

25 DIFFERENT VARIETIES OF FISH HAVE BEEN IDENTIFIED IN THE SEA OF GALILEE. THE ST PETER FISH IS VERY STRANGE. THE MALE CARRIES THE EGGS IN HIS LARGE MOUTH AND WHEN THE LITTLE FISH ARE BORN HE SPITS THEM OUT INTO THE WATER. AT THE LEAST SIGN OF DANGER THEY RETURN TO TAKE REFUGE IN THE FATHER'S MOUTH. TO DISSUADE THEM, HE FILLS HIS MOUTH WITH LITTLE STONES SO THAT THERE IS NO ROOM. BY TRADITION THIS COULD BE THE FISH MENTIONED IN MATTHEW 17. 24-27.

BOATS

BOATS AND NETS WERE EXPENSIVE, SO FISHERMEN FORMED CO-OPERATIVES OF SIX OR SEVEN PEOPLE. THEY HAD TO PAY A TAX TO HAVE THE RIGHT TO FISH IN A SPECIFIC PART OF THE LAKE. THE CO-OPERATIVES SOLD THE FISH TO TRADERS AND TO SPECIALISTS IN SALTING FISH (MAGDALA). PRESERVING FISH POSED PROBLEMS BECAUSE OF THE HIGH TEMPERATURES.

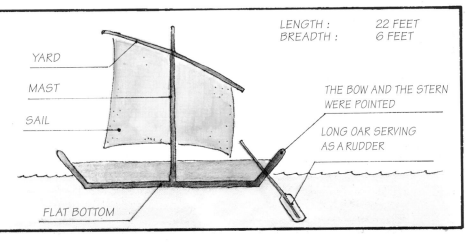

LENGTH : 22 FEET
BREADTH : 6 FEET

YARD

MAST

SAIL

THE BOW AND THE STERN WERE POINTED

LONG OAR SERVING AS A RUDDER

FLAT BOTTOM

SOUP, ALWAYS SOUP

I'M FED UP WITH SOUP

MUM HAS TOLD ME: 'ALL YOU'RE GETTING IS THREE OLIVES FOR DINNER!'

ER, IS THERE A BIT OF SOUP IN THE BOTTOM OF THE PAN?

EATING: WHAT, WHEN, HOW

IN A SOCIETY IN WHICH EATING ONE'S FILL WAS A REAL PROBLEM, SITTING DOWN TO A MEAL TOGETHER WAS AN IMPORTANT GESTURE TO SHOW FRIENDSHIP. STRANGERS AND ENEMIES COULD ALSO BE INVITED.* IN THE BIBLE, THE FIRST INVITATION TO A MEAL WITH AN INDICATION OF A MENU IS THE ONE ISSUED BY ABRAHAM AND SARAH TO THE MESSENGERS OF THE LORD (GENESIS 18. 6-8).

* WHEN IT WAS A MATTER OF LIFE AND DEATH

MEALS DURING THE DAY

BREAKFAST AS SUCH DIDN'T EXIST. CHILDREN HAD A LITTLE BUTTERMILK, THEIR PARENTS NIBBLED BREAD AND OLIVES ON THEIR WAY TO WORK.

DURING THE DAY PEOPLE HAD A QUICK BITE WITHOUT STOPPING WORK: BREAD AND CHEESE, FRESH OR DRIED FRUIT, MILK OR WINE DILUTED WITH WATER.

THE MAIN MEAL

WAS IN THE EVENING, AT SUNSET. THE FAMILY GATHERED AND ALL SAT ON MATS ON THE GROUND.

THE FOOD WAS SOUP, USUALLY A THICK SOUP MADE OF WHEAT, BARLEY, CHICK PEAS, BEANS AND LENTILS WHICH HAD SIMMERED FOR HOURS. WILD HERBS OR VEGETABLES AND SALT WERE ADDED.

THEY ATE EVERYTHING FROM THE SAME PLATE.

LOOK! Granny has made barley bread!

FISH OR MEAT WERE SERVED ONLY FOR THE SABBATH OR AT FESTIVALS.

10

A ROYAL DINNER
Menu
DUCK PATÉ WITH SESAME
STUFFED QUAILS WITH SEVEN SPICES
ONIONS IN HONEY
TURNIPS MARINATED IN WINE
ALMOND BISCUITS
APPLES FROM THE GARDEN OF EDEN
FRESH FRUIT
BREAD
WINE

A SIMPLER DINNER...

An ancient recipe

(WHICH STILL MAKES US LICK OUR LIPS...)

CHEESE

OLIVES

PISTACHIOS

CELERY

CAPERS

FOR 4 PERSONS:
- 1 CUP OF CURD CHEESE
- 6 GREEN AND 6 BLACK OLIVES STONED
  OR CUT IN STRIPS
- 1 SPOONFUL OF CHOPPED PISTACHIOS
  (NOT SALTED)
- 1 SPOONFUL OF CHOPPED CELERY
- 1 SPOONFUL OF CHOPPED CAPERS

MIX TOGETHER AND TURN OUT ON TO A PLATE.
DECORATE WITH PISTACHIOS AND CELERY.
SERVE WITH TOAST OR SALAD.

HOW THEY ATE

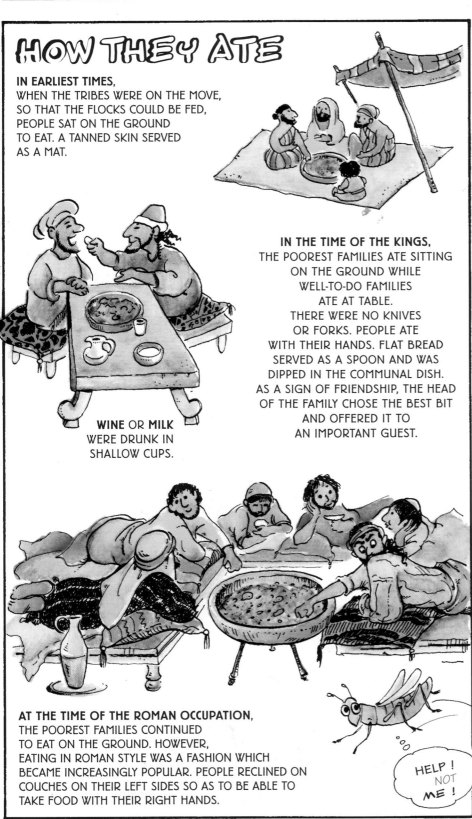

IN EARLIEST TIMES,
WHEN THE TRIBES WERE ON THE MOVE,
SO THAT THE FLOCKS COULD BE FED,
PEOPLE SAT ON THE GROUND
TO EAT. A TANNED SKIN SERVED
AS A MAT.

WINE OR **MILK**
WERE DRUNK IN
SHALLOW CUPS.

IN THE TIME OF THE KINGS,
THE POOREST FAMILIES ATE SITTING
ON THE GROUND WHILE
WELL-TO-DO FAMILIES
ATE AT TABLE.
THERE WERE NO KNIVES
OR FORKS. PEOPLE ATE
WITH THEIR HANDS. FLAT BREAD
SERVED AS A SPOON AND WAS
DIPPED IN THE COMMUNAL DISH.
AS A SIGN OF FRIENDSHIP, THE HEAD
OF THE FAMILY CHOSE THE BEST BIT
AND OFFERED IT TO
AN IMPORTANT GUEST.

AT THE TIME OF THE ROMAN OCCUPATION,
THE POOREST FAMILIES CONTINUED
TO EAT ON THE GROUND. HOWEVER,
EATING IN ROMAN STYLE WAS A FASHION WHICH
BECAME INCREASINGLY POPULAR. PEOPLE RECLINED ON
COUCHES ON THEIR LEFT SIDES SO AS TO BE ABLE TO
TAKE FOOD WITH THEIR RIGHT HANDS.

HELP !
NOT
ME !

IN PRAISE OF THE PUMPKIN

THE PUMPKIN IS
TASTY AND
NOURISHING.
DRIED, IT
CAN BE
USED AS
A VESSEL. PEOPLE
MADE BOWLS
FROM IT OR BIG
SPOONS FOR
EATING SOUP.

FORBIDDEN FOOD

IN THE BIBLE WE FIND RULES ABOUT
WHICH ANIMALS CAN BE EATEN.

*'Whatever parts the hoof and is cloven
footed and chews the cud among the
animals, you may eat'* (LEVITICUS 11.3).

CATTLE, SHEEP AND GOATS FALL INTO THIS
CATEGORY AND ARE THEREFORE CONSIDERED
CLEAN, **'KASHER'**, **I.E. PURE**.
OTHER ANIMALS LIKE THE CAMEL, PIG,
DONKEY ARE CONSIDERED **UNCLEAN**.
THE LIST OF CLEAN AND
UNCLEAN FOODS
IS VERY
LONG.

LUCKY FOR ME !

IN FACT GRASSHOPPERS WERE EATEN
FRIED, BOILED OR GRILLED AND TURNED
INTO FLOUR WHICH WAS RICH IN
CALORIES AND PROTEIN.

THE FAMILY

BIRTH

IN THE WORLD OF THE BIBLE THE BIRTH OF A CHILD WAS AN IMPORTANT EVENT, THE SOURCE OF GREAT JOY.

PREGNANT WOMEN HAD TO OBSERVE CERTAIN RULES. THEY COULD NOT TAKE HOT BATHS OR EAT FATTY OR SALTY FOOD FOR FEAR THAT IT MIGHT HARM THE CHILD. CHILDBIRTH USUALLY TOOK PLACE AT HOME, WITH THE HELP OF A MIDWIFE (EXODUS 1. 15–21). ALL CHILDREN WERE BREAST-FED BY THEIR MOTHER OR BY A WET-NURSE (I SAMUEL 1. 24) UNTIL THE AGE OF THREE. THERE WAS A BIG PARTY WHEN THE CHILD WAS WEANED.

ALL CHILDREN WERE A SOURCE OF JOY AT THIS TIME, BUT BOYS WERE THOUGHT A REAL BLESSING. THEY REMAINED IN THE FAMILY, WHICH GREW WHEN THEY HAD WIVES AND CHILDREN. BUT WHEN WOMEN MARRIED, THEY BECAME MEMBERS OF ANOTHER FAMILY.

THE PATRIARCHAL FAMILY

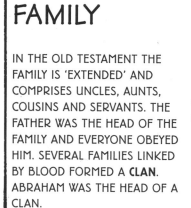

IN THE OLD TESTAMENT THE FAMILY IS 'EXTENDED' AND COMPRISES UNCLES, AUNTS, COUSINS AND SERVANTS. THE FATHER WAS THE HEAD OF THE FAMILY AND EVERYONE OBEYED HIM. SEVERAL FAMILIES LINKED BY BLOOD FORMED A **CLAN**. ABRAHAM WAS THE HEAD OF A CLAN.

A WELL-TO-DO FAMILY COULD GROW BY BUYING SLAVES. **SLAVES** WERE THE PROPERTY OF THEIR OWNERS BUT ENJOYED A PROTECTION WHICH WAS SCRUPULOUSLY SPELLED OUT. MASTERS GAVE THEIR SLAVES CONSIDERABLE RESPONSIBILITY. A MAN COULD HAVE LEGITIMATE CHILDREN BY SEVERAL WIVES AND ALSO BY SLAVES.

MARRIAGE

YOUNG PEOPLE DID NOT HAVE THE RIGHT TO CHOOSE WHOM THEY WANTED TO MARRY. THE FAMILIES DECIDED, AFTER LONG NEGOTIATIONS. IN FACT THEY HAD TO AGREE ON THE AMOUNT OF MONEY TO BE PAID TO THE BRIDE'S FATHER.

AT SUNSET THE BRIDEGROOM, ACCOMPANIED BY HIS FAMILY AND FRIENDS, GOES IN SEARCH OF THE BRIDE, TO HER PARENTS' HOUSE. THE BRIDE'S HEAD IS COVERED WITH A VEIL AND SHE GOES WITH HER FRIENDS TO THE BRIDEGROOM'S HOUSE. THE WAY IS LIT WITH TORCHES; THERE IS SINGING AND MUSIC.

ACCORDING TO AN OLD CUSTOM, SOME COINS FROM THIS SUM ARE HUNG ON HEADBANDS WORN BY THE BRIDE.
THE BETROTHAL LASTS FOR ABOUT A YEAR AND IS AS STRICT A COMMITMENT AS THE MARRIAGE ITSELF.

THE COUPLE ARE PLACED UNDER A CANOPY. THEY WEAR FINE CLOTHING AND JEWELS, LIKE A KING AND QUEEN, AND THE GUESTS EAT AND DRINK WITH GREAT REJOICING. THE CELEBRATIONS LAST A LONG TIME, UP TO A WEEK.

DEATH

WHEN SOMEONE DIES, THE FAMILY MEETS TO MOURN AND LAMENT. THE TEARS ARE A WAY OF TELLING THE NEIGHBORS THAT THERE IS A DEATH IN THE FAMILY. WELL-TO-DO FAMILIES PAID PEOPLE TO MOURN IN ORDER TO INTENSIFY THE LAMENTATION. TO EXPRESS MOURNING YOU TORE YOUR CLOTHING AND PUT ON GARMENTS OF SACKCLOTH.

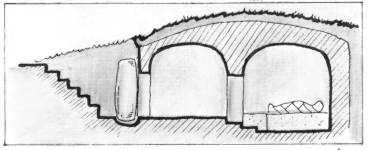

THE BODY WAS WRAPPED IN BANDAGES OR IN A SHROUD AND PUT IN A CAVE, NATURAL OR ARTIFICIAL. THE CAVE WAS ENLARGED AND NICHES HOLLOWED IN IT. THE OPENING WAS CLOSED BY A BIG STONE IN THE FORM OF A DISC WHICH COULD BE ROLLED IN A GROOVE, OR BY A SIMPLE ROCK. A WOMAN WHO SURVIVED HER HUSBAND WAS IN A DIFFICULT POSITION, AS SHE INHERITED NOTHING. THAT IS WHY THE LAW REQUIRES **WIDOWS** TO BE PROTECTED. **THE OLDEST SON** SUCCEEDED HIS FATHER, REPLACING HIM AS HEAD OF THE FAMILY AND AS A MEMBER OF THE CLAN.

IN ISRAEL, IN THE OLD DAYS, BOYS CAME OF AGE AT 13 . . .

GIRLS EVEN CAME OF AGE AT 12

AND COULD GET MARRIED!!

HOW DOES THIS BOW TIE SUIT ME?

CHILDREN

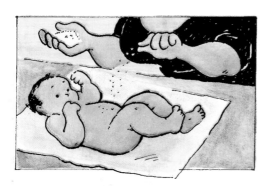

THE BIRTH OF A CHILD

ACCORDING TO THE BIBLE, CHILDREN ARE A PRECIOUS GIFT OF GOD GIVEN TO PARENTS. **THEY ARE THE FUTURE OF THE PEOPLE.**

CHILDREN WERE BORN AT HOME AS THERE WERE NO HOSPITALS. THE NEW-BORN BABY WAS WASHED AND RUBBED WITH SALT TO STRENGTHEN ITS SKIN. THEN THE MOTHER WRAPPED IT UP IN LITTLE BLANKETS AND PUT IT IN A HAMMOCK HUNG FROM THE CEILING.

THE LITTLE BLANKETS WERE CHANGED SEVERAL TIMES A DAY FOR HYGIENIC REASONS AND SO THAT THE BABY'S SKIN COULD BE RUBBED WITH OLIVE OIL. AS BABIES WERE WRAPPED UP, IT WAS EASIER TO CARRY THEM AROUND. MOTHERS WENT EVERYWHERE WITH THEIR BABIES AS THEY WERE BREAST-FEEDING THEM.

Another kind of hammock tied to posts in the form of a fork.

BOY BABIES HAD TO BE CIRCUMCISED ON THE EIGHTH DAY. IF THE BOY WAS THE FIRSTBORN, THE FAMILY HAD TO PAY FIVE PIECES OF SILVER TO THE PRIEST TO REDEEM HIM

(NUMBERS 18. 15–16).

NAME

AFTER BIRTH, EVERY CHILD RECEIVED A NAME, WHICH OFTEN HAD A PARTICULAR MEANING:

WE'LL CALL HIM **ESAU** (HAIRY)

RACHEL CALLED HER FIRST CHILD **JOSEPH** (MAY THE LORD ADD OTHER CHILDREN).

SARAH CALLED HER SON **ISAAC** (GOD HAS MADE ME LAUGH).

AT 13, BOYS CAME OF AGE AND COULD BE COUNTED AMONG THE TEN MEN NEEDED TO CONSTITUTE A SYNAGOGUE. GIRLS CAME OF AGE AT 12 AND COULD BE GIVEN IN MARRIAGE.

THE CHILD GROWS UP

FROM THEIR EARLIEST DAYS, GIRLS AND BOYS ARE PART OF THE PEOPLE OF ISRAEL. THEY JOIN IN WORSHIP IN THE FAMILY AND AT THE GREAT COMMUNAL FESTIVALS. CHILDREN GROW UP, AND LEARN THE HISTORY OF THEIR PEOPLE. BUT THEY ALSO LEARN TO KNOW THE LIVING LORD BY PRAYING AND WORKING WITH THEIR PARENTS. SCHOOLS DEVELOPED ONLY AROUND THE FIRST CENTURY BC.

UNFORTUNATELY THERE ARE ONLY NINE OF US MEN . . .

WAIT A MOMENT ! MY SON ABNER IS THIRTEEN NOW !

ADVICE TO PARENTS

THE BIBLE CONTAINS A BOOK CALLED **PROVERBS**. IT GIVES ADVICE FOR PARENTS WHICH IS 2500 YEARS OLD.

'Train a child in the way he should go, and when he is old he will not depart from it.'   22. 6

'Let your father and mother be glad, let her who bore you rejoice.'   23. 25

'Discipline your son and he will give you rest: he will give delight to your heart.'   29. 17

THUMBING THROUGH THE BIBLE...

THE WORD '**CHILD**' CAN MEAN . . .

CHILDREN USUALLY PLAYED OUTSIDE AS IT WAS DARK IN THE HOUSES. THEY RAN, JUMPED AND COMPETED IN IMITATING GROWN UPS.

GAMES

THEY HAD DICE, MARBLES AND TOPS; THEY THREW PEBBLES AND TRIED TO AIM ACCURATELY.

LITTLE TERRA COTTA OBJECTS HAVE BEEN FOUND WITH HOLES ON BOTH SIDES AND FILLED WITH SLIVERS OF CLAY. THESE WERE PROBABLY RATTLES FOR LITTLE ONES. GAMES LIKE HOPSCOTCH AND LUDO HAVE ALSO BEEN FOUND SCRATCHED ON STONE SURFACES.

AN UNIMPORTANT PERSON

Matthew 14.21

TODAY WE'VE FED 5000 MEN, NOT COUNTING THE WOMEN AND CHILDREN !

A SPECIAL PERSON

Mark 10.13-16

AN IDEAL WORLD

Isaiah 11.6

PEACE

'Like a child in its mother's arms, with you I have found silence and peace.'

Psalm 131.2

15

TEACHING

UP TO THE AGE OF THREE THE CHILDREN HAD THEIR FIRST EDUCATION FROM THEIR MOTHERS. THEN THE BOYS WERE TAUGHT THE LAW BY THEIR FATHERS. THE FATHER ALSO TAUGHT HIS SONS HIS OWN CRAFT. THE DAUGHTERS LEARNED FROM THEIR MOTHERS HOW TO KEEP HOUSE. THE BASIC INSTRUCTION WAS RELIGIOUS: PRAYERS REPEATED BY ADULTS WERE LEARNED BY HEART BY CHILDREN, AND THE FESTIVALS WITH THEIR RITES WERE AN OCCASION FOR THE NEW GENERATIONS TO LEARN WHAT THE LORD HAD DONE FOR HIS PEOPLE.

WHEN THE SANCTUARIES APPEARED, THOSE WHO WORKED THERE BEGAN TO TEACH IN A MORE SYSTEMATIC WAY (1 SAMUEL 1. 24). THE NUMBER OF PEOPLE WHO KNEW HOW TO READ AND WRITE INCREASED.

DURING THE EXILE IN BABYLON [6TH CENTURY] MUCH IMPORTANCE WAS ATTACHED TO KNOWLEDGE OF **THE LAW.** THE FIRST **SYNAGOGUES** WERE OPENED WHERE THE JEWS MET TO READ THE BIBLE.

AFTER THE EXILE CHILDREN OVER FIVE BEGAN TO GO **TO SCHOOL** TO LEARN TO **READ**, **WRITE** AND **COUNT**.

THE SCROLL OF SCRIPTURE WAS USED AS A **TEXTBOOK**.

THE **TEACHER** HAD TO BE A MARRIED MAN OF GOOD CHARACTER.

THE HEBREW ALPHABET

Aleph	א	1
Bet	ב	2
Gimel	ג	3
Daleth	ד	4
Hē	ה	5
Waw	ו	6
Zayin	ז	7
Heth	ח	8
Teth	ט	9
Yod	י	10

HEBREW IS WRITTEN FROM RIGHT TO LEFT. THE LETTERS OF THE ALPHABET ARE ONLY CONSONANTS. THE VOWELS ARE PRONOUNCED BUT NOT WRITTEN. EVERY LETTER ALSO CORRESPONDS TO A FIGURE.

WRITING MATERIAL

YOU COULD WRITE WITH A POINTED STYLUS ON A WAX-COVERED TABLET.

THE FLAT SIDE WAS USED FOR RUBBING OUT.

BITS OF CLAY (OSTRAKA) WERE MORE ECONOMICAL, PIECES OF BROKEN POT ON WHICH PEOPLE WROTE WITH INK.

PARCHMENT OR PAPYRUS WERE USED FOR WRITING MORE IMPORTANT THINGS.

INK WAS MADE WITH SOOT, RESIN, OIL AND WATER. THE PEN WAS A SHARPENED REED.

AND AFTERWARDS?

THE MOST BRILLIANT PUPILS COULD GO TO JERUSALEM TO STUDY WITH ONE OF THE GREAT MASTERS OF THE LAW (SCRIBES). ADULTS COULD GO ON LISTENING TO THE READING AND INTERPRETATION OF THE SCRIPTURES IN THE SYNAGOGUE.

WOMEN IN ISRAEL 1

IN ANTIQUITY IT WAS UNTHINKABLE FOR A WOMAN TO BE INDEPENDENT. IN OLD TESTAMENT TIMES, ALL OVER THE NEAR EAST, A WOMAN WAS CONSIDERED TO BE THE PROPERTY FIRST OF HER FATHER, THEN OF HER HUSBAND.

SO A WOMAN COULD **NOT** OWN ANYTHING, **NOR** BE A WITNESS, **NOR** TAKE PART IN PUBLIC LIFE. **HOWEVER**, MEMBERSHIP OF THE JEWISH PEOPLE DEPENDED ON THE MOTHER, NOT THE FATHER.

IF MALE GUESTS ARRIVE SHE STAYS IN THE HOUSE.

IN THE STREET SHE WALKS ON FOOT BEHIND HER HUSBAND.

SHE SERVES AT TABLE AND EATS AFTER THE MEN.

SHE GOES TO GET WATER, PREPARES THE MEAL AND MAKES CLOTHES FOR EVERYONE.

SHE HANDS DOWN THE TRADITIONS OF THE PAST TO HER CHILDREN.

CHILDREN

IN ISRAEL IT WAS THOUGHT IMPORTANT TO HAVE MANY CHILDREN. SO THE MOTHER'S ROLE WAS FUNDAMENTAL. NOT ONLY DID SHE GIVE BIRTH BUT ALSO SHE BROUGHT THEM UP, LOOKED AFTER THEM AND PROVIDED THEIR EDUCATION. EVERY MOTHER WAS THE FIRST TEACHER OF HER CHILDREN. SHE TAUGHT THEM TO LOVE AND RESPECT THE LORD, AND TO KNOW THE TRADITIONS OF THEIR PEOPLE.

THUMBING THROUGH THE BIBLE...

DESPITE HER INFERIOR POSITION, A WOMAN ENJOYED A DEGREE OF AUTONOMY IN EVERYDAY LIFE. WE DISCOVER THIS IN PROVERBS 31. 10-31.

A resourceful woman !

Here's Caleb. What a fine red linen tunic!

I'm sure his wife Milcah has made it. She's famous for her belts and garments. They're so good that she sells them to the merchants.

I discovered that last year she bought a splendid vineyard with the money she earned. She's made a good investment. What a lucky husband!

She also helps the poor. The whole town respects her for what she does.

There are many extraordinary women, but none like you !

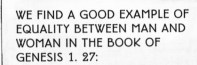

WE FIND A GOOD EXAMPLE OF EQUALITY BETWEEN MAN AND WOMAN IN THE BOOK OF GENESIS 1. 27:

'God created man in his image . . . He created them male and female . . .'

THE FAMILY IS MADE UP OF A LARGE NUMBER OF MEMBERS UNITED BY BONDS OF BLOOD. WHEN A WOMAN MARRIES, SHE ENTERS HER HUSBAND'S FAMILY. THERE SHE IS NOT FREE, BUT DOES ENJOY SOME PROTECTION.

FROM THE BOOK OF DEUTERONOMY

- IF A WOMAN IS LEFT A WIDOW, WITHOUT CHILDREN, THAT IS WITHOUT ANY MEANS OF SUPPORT, ONE OF HER HUSBAND'S BROTHERS MUST MARRY HER AND LOOK AFTER HER.

- A MAN MAY NOT DIVORCE HIS WIFE FOR TRIVIAL REASONS.

- IF A MAN HAS JUST MARRIED, HE MAY NOT GO OFF TO WAR OR BE CONSCRIPTED FOR OTHER WORK. FOR A YEAR HE SHALL BE ABLE TO DEVOTE HIMSELF TO HIS HOME AND THE HAPPINESS OF THE WOMAN HE HAS MARRIED.

FAMOUS WOMEN

MIRIAM, SISTER OF MOSES AND AARON, GOES WITH THE PEOPLE TOWARDS THE PROMISED LAND. SHE IS A PROPHETESS (EXODUS 15.20) WHO ENJOYS SOME PRESTIGE (MICAH 6. 4).

DEBORAH (JUDGES 4. 4-10) IS A PROPHETESS. IN OTHER WORDS, SHE PREACHES THE WORD OF GOD, ADMINISTERS JUSTICE AND ACCOMPANIES THE SOLDIERS TO BATTLE.

HULDAH (II KINGS 22. 14) THE PROPHETESS WAS CONSULTED BY KING JOSIAH. IT WAS A VERY IMPORTANT MOMENT FOR THE PEOPLE OF ISRAEL.

WOMEN IN ISRAEL 2

IN THE CITY

IN THE TIME OF JESUS, IN FAMILIES OF THE NOBILITY WHICH SCRUPULOUSLY OBSERVED THE LAW, BEFORE MARRIAGE YOUNG WOMEN REMAINED AT HOME AS LONG AS POSSIBLE. ONCE MARRIED, THEY ONLY WENT OUT IF THEIR HEADS WERE COVERED WITH A SPECIAL HEADDRESS.

POLITENESS DICTATED THAT MEN AVOIDED BEING ALONE WITH A WOMAN OR SPEAKING TO A MARRIED WOMAN ... EVEN LOOKING AT HER.

BY CONTRAST, AT THE COURT OF THE RULERS, LITTLE IMPORTANCE WAS ATTACHED TO CUSTOMS.

ORDINARY WOMEN COULD NOT LEAD THE SAME WITHDRAWN LIFE AS HIGH SOCIETY WOMEN. ABOVE ALL, FOR ECONOMIC REASONS, WOMEN HAD TO HELP THEIR HUSBANDS AT WORK, ALSO IN THE SHOPS. ORDINARY WOMEN COULD JOIN CHEERFULLY IN NIGHTLY FESTIVITIES DURING THE 'FEAST OF BOOTHS'.

IN THE COUNTRY RELATIONS BETWEEN PEOPLE WERE SIMPLER THAN IN TOWNS. WORK WAS HARDER AND REQUIRED AS MANY HANDS AS POSSIBLE.

IN THE COUNTRY

COUNTRY WOMEN WERE NOT SO STRICT ABOUT WEARING VEILS.

IN PALESTINE, AS THROUGHOUT THE NEAR EAST, GIRLS CAME OF AGE AROUND TWELVE AND MARRIED EARLY. BEFORE MARRIAGE CAME BETROTHAL AND THE DRAFTING OF A MARRIAGE CONTRACT IN WHICH THE COMPENSATION TO BE PAID IN THE CASE OF A SEPARATION WAS FIXED. FROM THAT MOMENT ON THE ENGAGED WOMAN WAS CALLED 'BRIDE'. AS SUCH SHE COULD BE PUT TO DEATH FOR ADULTERY.

MARRIED WOMEN WORKED IN THE FIELDS WITH THEIR HUSBANDS AND CHILDREN. HOWEVER, A WOMAN COULD NOT BE ALONE IN THE COUNTRY. EVEN IN THE COUNTRY A MAN WOULD RARELY SPEAK TO A STRANGER.

WOMEN MAKE THEIR PURCHASES IN THE VILLAGE MARKETS.

WOMEN GO FROM DOOR TO DOOR SELLING OLIVES.

YOUNG GIRLS GO TO GET WATER FROM THE FOUNTAIN OR WELL.

WHAT CRAFTSMAN-SHIP !

CRAFTS 1

Hey ! Ephraim, listen . . . .

Can't stop! Next time

THE SMELL OF TREATING HIDES WAS SO UNPLEASANT THAT THE TANNER HAD TO WORK OUTSIDE THE TOWN.

SCRAPING

DRYING

SOAKING IN DOGS' EXCREMENT

LEATHER

ORIGINALLY THE TENTS OF NOMADS WERE MADE WITH HIDES. LATER, THE HIDES WERE REPLACED WITH GOATS' HAIR FABRIC. SO TENTMAKERS WERE CRAFTSMEN IN LEATHER, TANNERS. THE NAME REMAINED EVEN WHEN THE LEATHER WAS USED TO MAKE OTHER OBJECTS.

PARCHMENT

SANDAL

CONTAINER FOR LIQUIDS

SHIELD

BELT

THE TOOLS

MALLET

CHISEL

HAMMER

PLUMB LINE

RULE AND SQUARE FOR MEASURING

STONE

BLOCKS OF STONE WERE GOT FROM QUARRIES AND CUT DOWN TO THE DESIRED SIZE. THE STONES WERE THEN TRANSPORTED TO THE WORKSHOP AND RE-CUT BY STONE-CUTTERS. ONLY THE MOST IMPORTANT BUILDINGS WERE MADE OF STONE.

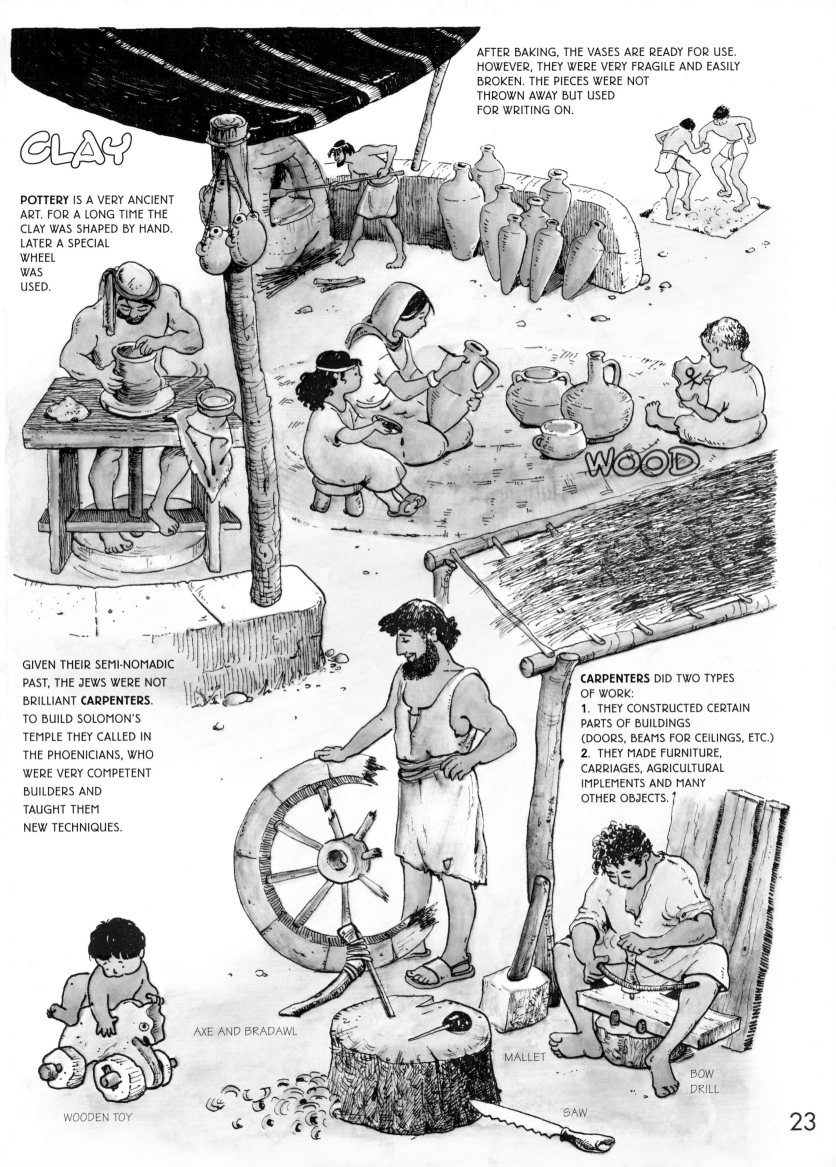

CLAY

POTTERY IS A VERY ANCIENT ART. FOR A LONG TIME THE CLAY WAS SHAPED BY HAND. LATER A SPECIAL WHEEL WAS USED.

AFTER BAKING, THE VASES ARE READY FOR USE. HOWEVER, THEY WERE VERY FRAGILE AND EASILY BROKEN. THE PIECES WERE NOT THROWN AWAY BUT USED FOR WRITING ON.

WOOD

GIVEN THEIR SEMI-NOMADIC PAST, THE JEWS WERE NOT BRILLIANT CARPENTERS. TO BUILD SOLOMON'S TEMPLE THEY CALLED IN THE PHOENICIANS, WHO WERE VERY COMPETENT BUILDERS AND TAUGHT THEM NEW TECHNIQUES.

CARPENTERS DID TWO TYPES OF WORK:
1. THEY CONSTRUCTED CERTAIN PARTS OF BUILDINGS (DOORS, BEAMS FOR CEILINGS, ETC.)
2. THEY MADE FURNITURE, CARRIAGES, AGRICULTURAL IMPLEMENTS AND MANY OTHER OBJECTS.

WOODEN TOY

AXE AND BRADAWL

MALLET

SAW

BOW DRILL

ONCE, MEN WERE THE CRAFTSMEN

WOMEN ONLY DID SPINNING AND WEAVING

HAPPILY, TIMES HAVE CHANGED

MACHINES DO THE CRAFTSMANSHIP, AND THE SPINNING AND WEAVING!

CRAFTS 2

METAL

FROM EARLIEST TIMES THE JEWS HAVE BEEN VERY SKILFUL AT MAKING LITTLE **GOLD** OBJECTS. **GOLD** IS REFINED BY HEATING IT TO MELTING POINT IN CLAY VESSELS. THE IMPURITIES WHICH APPEAR ON THE SURFACE ARE REMOVED.

ANCIENT OVEN FOR MELTING GOLD

BLACKSMITH BEATING IRON

CRAFTSMEN POURING METAL INTO A MOULD FOR AN AXE

HIGH TEMPERATURE OVEN FOR WELDING **BRONZE**

IRON IS HARD TO WORK BECAUSE IT NEEDS VERY HIGH TEMPERATURES. ISRAEL HAD SOME DIFFICULT MOMENTS WHEN NEIGHBOURING PEOPLE BEGAN TO USE IRON IN MAKING WEAPONS.

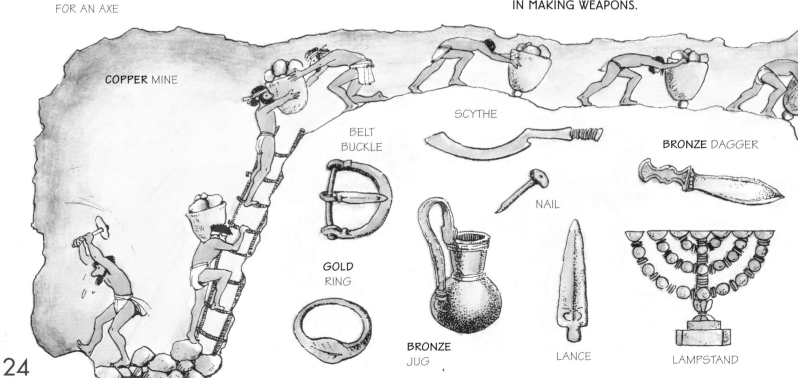

COPPER MINE

BELT BUCKLE

SCYTHE

BRONZE DAGGER

NAIL

GOLD RING

BRONZE JUG

LANCE

LAMPSTAND

MARKET DAY

MANY COUNTRY PRODUCTS WERE TAKEN TO JERUSALEM, ABOVE ALL AT FESTIVAL TIMES, WHEN LARGE NUMBERS OF PILGRIMS FLOCKED IN..

THE MERCHANDISE IS PUT ON THE GROUND AND THE SELLER SITS IN THE MIDDLE OF IT. PRICES ARE RARELY FIXED. THERE IS LONG HAGGLING OVER EVERY TRANSACTION. PAYMENT IS MADE IN KIND (ONE TYPE OF GOODS FOR ANOTHER) OR WITH METAL OR COINS..

COINS AND MEASURES

MANY COINS CIRCULATED IN THE COUNTRY AND PEOPLE DID NOT ALWAYS KNOW THEIR REAL VALUE.

 1 SILVER DENARIUS (ROMAN COINAGE)

 1 SILVER DRACHMA (GREEK COINAGE)

 1 SILVER SHEKEL (TEMPLE COINAGE)

MEASURES OF LENGTH WERE FIXED BY THE HUMAN BODY. FOR EXAMPLE, THE **CUBIT** WAS THE LENGTH OF THE FOREARM.

18 Inches

SOLID **MEASURES** DIFFERED FROM LIQUID MEASURES. THE **BATH** WAS USED FOR OIL AND WINE, THE **EPHAH** FOR WHEAT, BARLEY, ETC. 10 EPHAHS MADE AN **OMER** (THE AMOUNT AN ASS COULD CARRY).

MONEY CHANGERS WERE NEEDED WHEN A PRECISE SUM HAD TO BE PAID. FOR EXAMPLE, THE TEMPLE OFFERING HAD TO BE PAID IN SHEKELS.

PRAISE FOR THE ASS

HE CAN CARRY A PERSON FOR A DAY AND TROT FOR HOURS. ON SLOPES AND STEEP GROUND HE IS BETTER THAN A HORSE. THE WEIGHT HE CAN CARRY HAS GIVEN ITS NAME TO A UNIT OF MEASURE: THE OMER.

27

OIL AND BREAD

A MEDITERRANEAN RECIPE, SIMPLE AND ANCIENT

NOTHING SO MODERN AND COMPLICATED AS SOUP!

BREAD AND OIL

FLOUR IS MIXED WITH **WATER** AND **SALT**. A LITTLE OF YESTERDAY'S DOUGH IS ADDED AND THE MIXTURE IS ALLOWED TO REST.

AS IT **RISES**, THE DOUGH PRODUCES BUBBLES. THAT MAKES IT LIGHTER AND EASIER TO KNEAD AND DIGEST.

VARIOUS KINDS OF BREAD ARE MENTIONED IN THE BIBLE: LEAVENED AND UNLEAVENED, WITH OIL, BUNS, DOUGHNUTS.

IN THE TEMPLE, BREAD WAS OFFERED AS A SACRIFICE, BUT IT COULD NOT BE LEAVENED AND IT HAD TO BE MADE WITH A VERY FINE FLOUR (LEVITICUS 24. 5-9). UNLEAVENED BREAD, WITHOUT YEAST, WAS EATEN AT PASSOVER.

BREAD AND **OIL** HAVE ALWAYS BEEN THE BASIC FOOD OF MEDITERRANEAN PEOPLE. IN EVERY JEWISH FAMILY, BREAD WAS MADE FOR THE DAY EVERY MORNING. THE HEAVY WORK OF MILLING WAS LEFT TO THE WOMEN, WHO GOT UP BEFORE DAWN TO TURN THE GRAIN INTO COARSE FLOUR. **FLOUR** COULD ALSO BE MADE FROM BARLEY, WHICH WAS MUCH CHEAPER.

THE DOUGH IS SHAPED AND THEN PUT IN THE **OVEN**. THERE WERE SEVERAL KINDS OF OVEN.

THE DIFFERENT KINDS OF BREAD

Twelve loaves were offered every sabbath.

MILLS

DOMESTIC MILLS CAME IN TWO SIZES. TWO PEOPLE WERE NEEDED TO TURN THE BIGGEST.

Turning millstone *Fixed millstone* *Fabric on which flour falls*

AT CAPERNAUM, ARCHAEOLOGISTS HAVE FOUND A **STONE MILL IN THE SHAPE OF A BELL**, MORE THAN SIX FEET HIGH. IT WAS USED BY THE MERCHANTS OR BAKERS IN THE LARGE TOWNS.

THUMBING THROUGH THE BIBLE

THE LOW RAINFALL OFTEN LED TO SHORTAGES WHICH HIT THE POPULATION. THERE IS FREQUENT TALK OF FAMINE IN BOTH OLD AND NEW TESTAMENTS. THAT IS WHY IN MANY PASSAGES IN THE BIBLE BREAD IS PRESENTED AS THE SYMBOL OF LIFE AND IS GIVEN BY GOD.

EXODUS 16. 15–16

MARK 6. 30–34

JESUS OFTEN USES THE IMAGE OF BREAD IN HIS PARABLES AND SPEAKS OF HIMSELF AS THE 'BREAD OF LIFE' (JOHN 6. 35).

OLIVE TREES ARE WIDESPREAD IN PALESTINE. IN OCTOBER THE OLIVES ARE BROUGHT DOWN BY KNOCKING THE BRANCHES WITH STICKS. THE OLIVES ARE PRESSED IN A **PRESS** ACTUALLY IN THE OLIVE GROVE. THE CRUSHED PULP IS THEN PRESSED TO EXTRACT THE **OIL**. THIS IS TRANSFERRED TO TERRA COTTA JARS AND KEPT COOL.

Oil jar.
A small jug is put in the mouth so that when the oil is poured out the drops are collected in the jar.

BECAUSE OF THEIR NUMEROUS USES IN EVERYDAY LIFE, OLIVES WERE MUCH PRIZED.

THE TREE OF LIFE

IN FOOD

KEPT BY SALTING IT, THE FRUIT CONTAINS VITAMINS, PROTEINS AND FATS. PEASANTS LIKED BREAD AND OLIVES FOR ORDINARY BREAKFAST.

It is said that at Massada, a fortress besieged by the Romans, when they ran out of food the inhabitants managed to go on resisting by each eating seven olives a day.

AS A COSMETIC

OIL MADE HAIR SHINE AND SKIN SUPPLE. NOT TO ANOINT THE BODY WAS A SIGN OF SORROW. AS A PERFUMED OINTMENT, OIL REACHED EXORBITANT PRICES: IN THE JERUSALEM MARKET A FLASK OF 5–10 CL COST BETWEEN 150 AND 300 PIECES OF SILVER.

FOR LIGHTING

OH! THE OIL HAS ALMOST RUN OUT

IN MEDICINE

INFANTS AND THE WOUNDED WERE MASSAGED WITH OLIVE OIL (LUKE 10.34).

IN BURIALS

THE DEAD PERSON WAS SMEARED WITH OIL AND SPRINKLED WITH PERFUME (MARK 16. 1).

IN TRADE

ABROAD, OIL FROM GALILEE WAS MUCH PRIZED AND WAS VERY EXPENSIVE.

ONLY OIL FROM THE FIRST PRESSING WAS USED IN THE GREAT LAMPSTAND OF THE TEMPLE AS IT WAS THE BEST QUALITY (EXODUS 27. 20).

FOR SACRIFICES

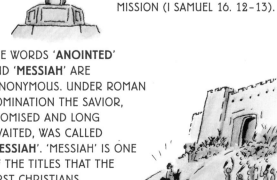

OIL WAS KEPT IN THE SANCTUARY TO CONSECRATE **PRIESTS, PROPHETS** AND **KINGS**, TO SHOW THAT THESE MEN WERE DEDICATED TO GOD AND SET APART FOR A SPECIAL MISSION (I SAMUEL 16. 12–13).

THE WORDS '**ANOINTED**' AND '**MESSIAH**' ARE SYNONYMOUS. UNDER ROMAN DOMINATION THE SAVIOR, PROMISED AND LONG AWAITED, WAS CALLED '**MESSIAH**'. 'MESSIAH' IS ONE OF THE TITLES THAT THE FIRST CHRISTIANS BESTOWED ON JESUS. '**CHRIST**' IS THE GREEK TRANSLATION OF THE HEBREW 'MESSIAH'.

29

WHY ARE YOU IN SUCH A GOOD HUMOR, BEN?

DID YOU GET AN A IN MATHS?

NO ...

ARE YOU IN LOVE?

NO ...

TODAY, TEACHER TOOK US ON A TRIP TO THE LOCAL WINE CELLARS!

BLVRP

VINES AND WINE

*A man is going to **his** vineyard ...*

*but is it **his**?*

THE OWNERSHIP OF THE EARTH

FOR THE PEOPLE OF ISRAEL THE LORD IS THE ONLY OWNER OF ALL CREATION. SO THE EARTH IS THE LORD'S, WHO GIVES IT AS A HERITAGE TO FAMILIES, CLANS, TRIBES. TO SELL ONE'S HERITAGE IS A LACK OF RESPECT TOWARDS GOD. IT IS ALLOWED ONLY IN CASES OF GRAVE NECESSITY. AT ALL EVENTS, LAND MUST BE RETURNED TO ITS ORIGINAL OWNERS IN THE YEAR OF JUBILEE (EVERY FIFTY YEARS, LEVITICUS 25. 13–17). THE LAND IS HANDED DOWN FROM FATHER TO SON. THE OLDEST SON RECEIVES TWICE AS MUCH AS HIS BROTHERS. ONLY IN THE ABSENCE OF MALE HEIRS IS THE INHERITANCE HANDED ON TO DAUGHTERS.

PLANTING A VINE

1 Vines are planted on hillsides, well exposed to the sun.

2 The stones are cleared.

3 The stones are used to make terraces which are surrounded with a wall and a ditch.
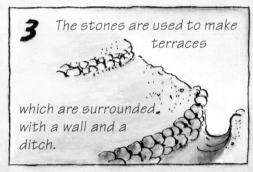

4 A thorn hedge is planted on the top of the wall to keep out wild animals.

5 Then a tower is built for the family to live in for the summer. At harvest time the top floor was used to keep an eye on the vineyard.

6 Building a tower was expensive. Those who couldn't afford it contented themselves with a tent or cabin.

7 When everything is ready the vines are planted about twelve feet apart to allow them to grow.

8 In March, the shoots are pruned

What about thieves? The law allows people to take a few bunches but not whole basketsful.

THE GRAPE HARVEST

IT BEGAN IN JULY AND LASTED UNTIL SEPTEMBER. THE WHOLE VILLAGE WENT TO THE VINEYARD, AS THERE WAS LOTS OF WORK. ALTHOUGH THEY WERE TIRED, DURING THE GRAPE HARVEST PEOPLE SANG, ORGANIZED FESTIVALS AND DANCED.

SOME GRAPES WERE EATEN FRESH OR PRESSED TO MAKE GRAPE JUICE. SOME OF THE GRAPES WERE DRIED. SOME OF THE JUICE WAS BOILED TO MAKE A THICK SWEET SYRUP.

WINE WAS A VERY COMMON DRINK. IT WENT WITH MEALS AND WAS ALWAYS DRUNK AT FESTIVALS. THE BIBLE CONDEMNS THE ABUSE OF WINE BUT NEVER DRINKING IT.

GRAPES WERE PRESSED IN A VAT. THIS WAS A BASIN HOLLOWED OUT IN THE ROCK WITH A DRAIN WHICH MADE IT POSSIBLE TO COLLECT THE JUICE IN A LOWER VAT. IN THE VAT SEVERAL PEOPLE TOGETHER PRESSED THE GRAPES WITH BURSTS OF LAUGHTER AND GENERAL GOOD HUMOR.

TO GET WINE, THE GRAPE JUICE HAD TO BE FERMENTED FOR ABOUT SIX WEEKS. THE WINE WAS THEN CAREFULLY TRANSFERRED TO WELL-SEALED CLAY AMPHORAS. A HOLE WAS LEFT NEAR THE NECK TO ALLOW THE GAS FROM THE FERMENTATION TO ESCAPE. WHEN THE FERMENTATION ENDED, THE HOLE WAS STOPPED UP WITH FRESH CLAY.

WINE CAN HAVE A SPECIAL SIGNIFICANCE

DURING THE CELEBRATION OF **PASSOVER**, THE CUPS OF WINE MARK THE MOMENTS WHEN THANKS IS GIVEN TO THE LORD WHO FREED HIS PEOPLE. AT THE BEGINNING OF THE **SABBATH** MEAL THE HEAD OF THE FAMILY RAISES A CUP OF WINE AND BLESSES THE LORD'S DAY.

THE LORD'S VINEYARD

THIS EXPRESSION DENOTES THE PEOPLE OF ISRAEL. ISRAEL IS GOD'S VINEYARD IN WHICH HE HAS WORKED, CLEARING THE STONES TO PLANT CHOICE VINES IN IT, FROM WHICH FRUIT IS EXPECTED (PSALM 80 AND ISAIAH 5. 1–7). FRIEZES DEPICTING BUNCHES OF GRAPES CAN OFTEN BE SEEN ABOVE THE ENTRANCES TO SYNAGOGUES.

Frieze from the synagogue in Capernaum

31

HOUSES BIG AND SMALL

Roman 'insula' at Caesarea

DURING THE ROMAN OCCUPATION OF ISRAEL, LUXURIOUS BUILDINGS IMITATED THE GRAECO-ROMAN STYLE. THE VILLA WAS SPACIOUS, WELL-PROPORTIONED AND WELL-PROTECTED. HOUSES WERE NOT AS COMFORTABLE AS OURS TODAY, BUT SERVANTS BUSTLED ABOUT SO THAT THEIR MASTERS COULD RELAX. EVEN THE BUILDINGS HOUSING THE LESS WELL-TO-DO WERE BUILT LIKE THOSE IN ROME. THEY WERE ENORMOUS STRUCTURES WITH NO RUNNING WATER. THE INHABITANTS WERE CRAMMED IN, TO THE NOISE OF SHOUTING, LAUGHTER AND QUARRELS.

THE ROOF IS MADE OF BEAMS, BRANCHES AND EARTH

FRUIT IS DRIED

THE ROOF IS ALSO A COOL PLACE WHERE PEOPLE CHAT IN THE EVENING

MATS FOR LYING ON

OIL LAMP

BRICKS OF MUD AND GRAVEL

RAISED LEVEL FOR THE FAMILY

THERE IS NO CHIMNEY

STONE FOUNDATION

STABLE OF BEATEN EARTH

UNDERGROUND STORE FOR FOOD

THE DOORWAY IS LOW

THERE ARE NO TOILETS

LITTLE CISTERN FOR RAIN WATER

UPSTAIRS ROOM FOR GUESTS

THERE IS NO RUNNING WATER

TERRA COTTA RECEPTACLE HOLDING WATER FOR RITUAL ABLUTIONS

ROLLER FOR FLATTENING THE ROOF AFTER RAIN

JUST ONE SMALL, HIGH WINDOW WITHOUT GLASS

In houses in Israel there was only one room

for cooking, eating and sleeping

Even the animals lived in it

FORTUNATELY THEY DIDN'T ALSO HAVE TO FIT IN THE FRIDGE, THE TV, THE WASHING MACHINE, THE DISHWASHER, THE MICROWAVE, THE COMPUTER ...

IN THE HOUSE

SMALL HEARTHS FOR PREPARING FOOD

COOKING WAS USUALLY DONE OUTSIDE, BUT IN BAD WEATHER FOOD WAS PREPARED INSIDE. THERE WAS NO CHIMNEY AND THE LITTLE ROOM WAS SOON FILLED WITH SMOKE.

PEOPLE SLEPT FULLY DRESSED, WITH THEIR CLOAKS AS BLANKETS, ON MATS LAID ON THE GROUND IN THE RAISED PART OF THE HOUSE.

MAT

CLOTHES CHEST

THE ANIMALS WERE BROUGHT IN AT NIGHT AND SLEPT IN THE LOWER PART OF THE HOUSE.

MILL

SHOPPING BAG AND BASKET MADE OF PALM FRONDS

WOODEN SPOON

THE HOUSES WERE SO DARK THAT THE OIL LAMP WAS LIT ALL DAY.

BROOM

STONE AND MORTAR AND PESTLE

TERRA COTTA JARS AND UTENSILS

PROVISIONS WERE KEPT UNDER THE HOUSE IN CAVES HOLLOWED OUT IN THE DARK.

IT WAS PUT AS HIGH AS POSSIBLE TO ILLUMINATE THE WHOLE ROOM.

THIS IS WHAT WE FIND IN A RICH MERCHANT'S HOUSE, BUILT IN THE ROMAN STYLE WITH COURTYARDS, GARDENS, WATER AND LIGHT IN ABUNDANCE.

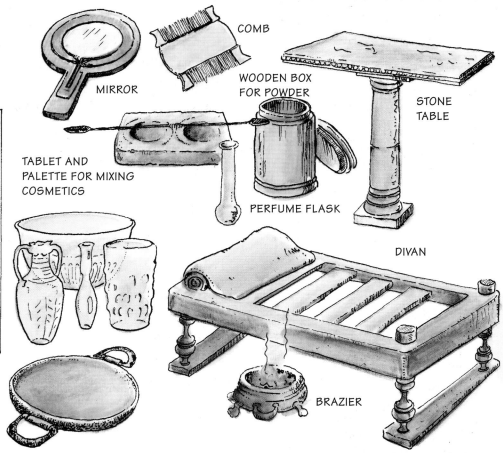

MIRROR

COMB

WOODEN BOX FOR POWDER

STONE TABLE

TABLET AND PALETTE FOR MIXING COSMETICS

PERFUME FLASK

DIVAN

STONE, BRONZE AND GLASS VESSELS

BRAZIER

CLOTHING

MOST PEOPLE HAD FEW CLOTHES AND HAD TO MAKE THEM LAST A LONG TIME. FESTAL GARMENTS WERE EXPENSIVE AND WERE HANDED DOWN FROM FATHER TO SON.

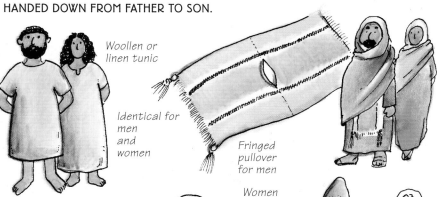

Woollen or linen tunic

Identical for men and women

Fringed pullover for men

The cloak gave protection from the sun and the rain. The poor also used it as a blanket.

When working, men pulled up their tunics and tucked them into their belts.

Women always covered their hair with a veil.

The clothing of the rich was made of fine fabrics. Men wore light cloaks with long fringes.

Men protected themselves from the sun with a scarf.

SHOES

SHOES WERE VERY EXPENSIVE. AT HOME PEOPLE WENT AROUND IN BARE FEET, BUT NO ONE WOULD THINK OF GOING OUT WITHOUT SANDALS. ONLY PEOPLE IN MOURNING AND SLAVES WENT OUT BAREFOOT.

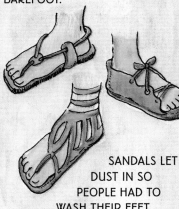

SANDALS LET DUST IN SO PEOPLE HAD TO WASH THEIR FEET BEFORE GOING INSIDE. THIS WAS THE JOB OF A SLAVE, OR THE MASTER OF THE HOUSE AS A SIGN OF RESPECT TO HIS GUEST.

Stone basin found in a well-to-do house in Jerusalem.

Foot rest

Hole to let the water out

TWO KINDS OF PURSE

The tunic, pulled up and tucked into its belt, forms a pocket.

Fabric or leather bag hung from the belt

JEWELS

Necklaces

Ear rings

Belt buckle

Bracelets

Ring

Jewelbox

35

IN BIBLICAL TIMES, IN THE VILLAGES IT WAS COLD AND WET IN WINTER

AND SMELLY IN SUMMER

IN MY TOWN IT'S COLD AND WET IN WINTER AND SMELLY ALL YEAR ROUND

TOWNS AND VILLAGES

MEGIDDO

A **FORTIFIED** CITY ON THE SLOPES OF MOUNT CARMEL, WHICH DOMINATES THE RICH PLAIN CROSSED BY THE ROAD FROM EGYPT TO SYRIA. THE SIGNIFICANCE OF THE CITY IS DUE TO ITS STRATEGIC POSITION. THIS HAS BEEN CONFIRMED BY ARCHAEOLOGISTS, WHO HAVE FOUND TWENTY LEVELS OF DWELLINGS. AT THE LOWEST LEVEL EXPERTS HAVE RECONSTRUCTED THIS MODEL OF THE CITY AS IT PROBABLY WAS IN THE TIME OF KING AHAB OF ISRAEL IN THE NINTH CENTURY BC.

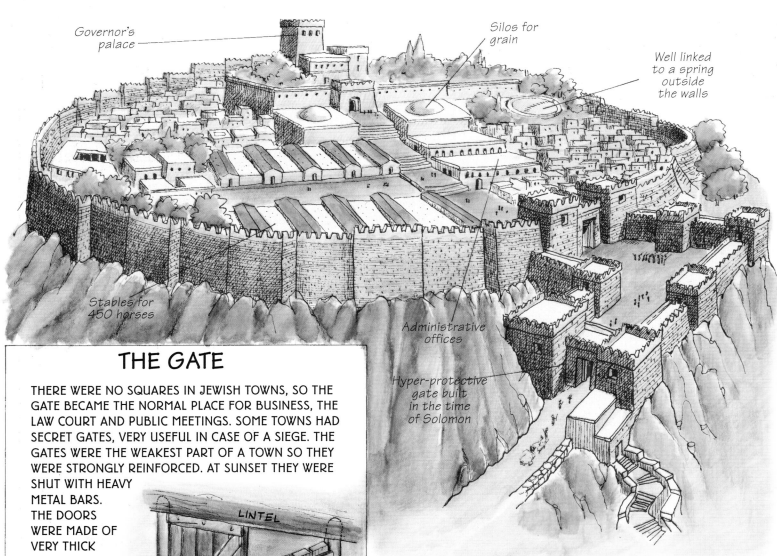

Governor's palace

Silos for grain

Well linked to a spring outside the walls

Stables for 450 horses

Administrative offices

Hyper-protective gate built in the time of Solomon

THE GATE

THERE WERE NO SQUARES IN JEWISH TOWNS, SO THE GATE BECAME THE NORMAL PLACE FOR BUSINESS, THE LAW COURT AND PUBLIC MEETINGS. SOME TOWNS HAD SECRET GATES, VERY USEFUL IN CASE OF A SIEGE. THE GATES WERE THE WEAKEST PART OF A TOWN SO THEY WERE STRONGLY REINFORCED. AT SUNSET THEY WERE SHUT WITH HEAVY METAL BARS. THE DOORS WERE MADE OF VERY THICK WOOD COVERED WITH BRONZE. THE POSTS PIVOTED AT THE TOP IN THE LINTEL AND AT THE BOTTOM ON PIERCED STONES.

LINTEL

CITIES WERE ALWAYS PROTECTED BY WALLS AND SITUATED NEAR SPRINGS OR CISTERNS. THEY WERE ECONOMIC, CULTURAL AND RELIGIOUS CENTERS. THEY CAN BE DIVIDED INTO THREE CATEGORIES:
1. **THE ROYAL CAPITALS:** LIKE SAMARIA AND JERUSALEM.
2. **THE ADMINISTRATIVE CENTERS:** MUCH IMPORTANCE WAS ATTACHED TO WAREHOUSES, OFFICES AND THE GOVERNOR'S RESIDENCE (AS AT LACHISH AND MEGIDDO). THERE WERE ALSO SMALLER ADMINISTRATIVE CENTRES LIKE BEERSHEBA.
3. **FORTIFIED PROVINCIAL TOWNS:** THESE HAD NO PUBLIC BUILDINGS. THE HOUSES WERE STUCK TOGETHER IN NO ORDER.

A VILLAGE

THE CHOICE OF SITE DEPENDED ON THE FERTILITY OF THE GROUND AND THE PRESENCE OF A WATER SUPPLY.

AFTER THE EXILE, SYNAGOGUES WERE BUILT EVERYWHERE, PROVIDED THAT THERE WERE AT LEAST TEN MEN.

THE MARKET WAS NEAR THE GATE. THE GATE WAS ALSO A PLACE OF DISCUSSION AND CHAT.

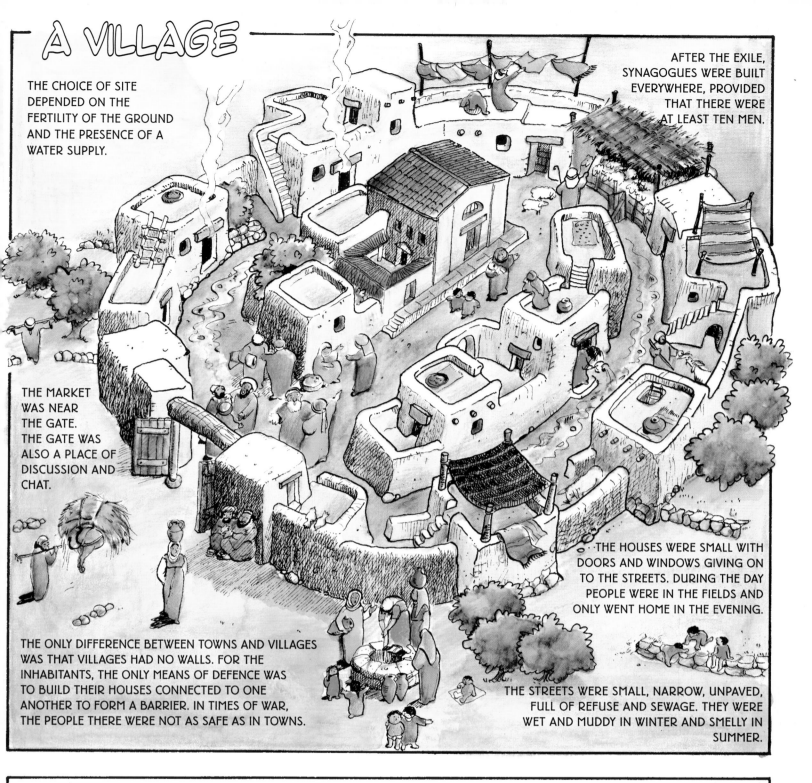

THE HOUSES WERE SMALL WITH DOORS AND WINDOWS GIVING ON TO THE STREETS. DURING THE DAY PEOPLE WERE IN THE FIELDS AND ONLY WENT HOME IN THE EVENING.

THE ONLY DIFFERENCE BETWEEN TOWNS AND VILLAGES WAS THAT VILLAGES HAD NO WALLS. FOR THE INHABITANTS, THE ONLY MEANS OF DEFENCE WAS TO BUILD THEIR HOUSES CONNECTED TO ONE ANOTHER TO FORM A BARRIER. IN TIMES OF WAR, THE PEOPLE THERE WERE NOT AS SAFE AS IN TOWNS.

THE STREETS WERE SMALL, NARROW, UNPAVED, FULL OF REFUSE AND SEWAGE. THEY WERE WET AND MUDDY IN WINTER AND SMELLY IN SUMMER.

CAESAREA, A ROMAN CITY

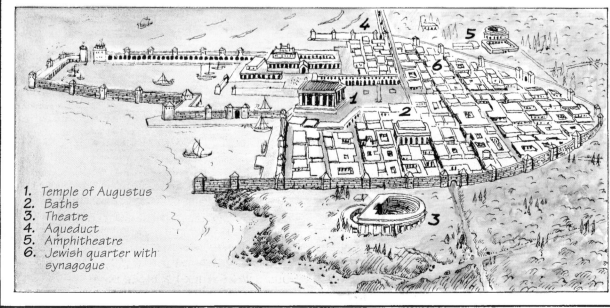

1. Temple of Augustus
2. Baths
3. Theatre
4. Aqueduct
5. Amphitheatre
6. Jewish quarter with synagogue

BUILT IN 22 BC BY HEROD THE GREAT, IT WAS THE CHIEF CITY OF OCCUPIED PALESTINE, AN IMPORTANT HUB OF ROADS AND A DYNAMIC TRADING PORT. IT WAS BUILT ON THE ROMAN MODEL WITH A PAVED MAIN ROAD ALONG WHICH WERE SHOPS, THEATRES AND PUBLIC BATHS. IT HAD A SEWAGE SYSTEM WHICH KEPT IT CLEAN. ITS PORT, NOW UNDER WATER, IS STILL STUDIED BY ARCHAEOLOGISTS.

YOU'RE ALWAYS THERE. YOU NEVER GET AWAY FROM THE TV

DON'T YOU WANT TO MEET NEW PEOPLE, DISCOVER NEW PLACES, TRAVEL?

LET'S GO, BABY!

TRAVEL

SAILING

FOR JEWS IN EARLIEST TIMES THE SEA REPRESENTED THE END OF THE WORLD. IT WAS THOUGHT EXTREMELY DANGEROUS. SAILING WAS A VIRTUAL MONOPOLY OF THE PHOENICIANS.

AT THE TIME OF THE ROMAN CONQUEST, SEA VOYAGES BECAME INCREASINGLY FREQUENT. THE MEDITERRANEAN WAS CRISS-CROSSED BY GREEK, ROMAN AND CARTHAGINIAN BOATS.

A ROMAN MERCHANT SHIP
THERE ARE NO ROWERS. ALL THE SPACE IS USED FOR CARGO.

SEVERAL TYPES OF ANCHOR

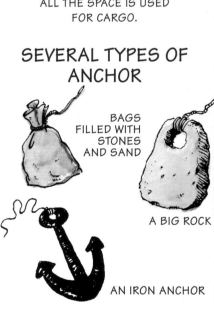

BAGS FILLED WITH STONES AND SAND

A BIG ROCK

AN IRON ANCHOR

POOR TRAVELLERS

Almost always, the passengers were simply added to the merchandise transported.

They had to take their own food.

PUF PUF

At night they had to return to land.

For safety reasons the ships did not sail far from shore, so voyages took a very long time.

SHIP WRECKS

BUT WHAT MONTH ARE WE IN?

NOTICE TO SAILORS
The law forbids sailing between 10 November and 10 March

THE LARGE NUMBER OF OBJECTS RECOVERED FROM THE BOTTOM OF THE MEDITERRANEAN PROVE THAT SHIPWRECKS WERE VERY FREQUENT.

TRAVEL BY LAND

FROM THE DAWN OF TIME, THE ROADS IN ISRAEL WERE RUDIMENTARY. FULL OF HOLES AND STONES, THEY WERE TRAVELLED BY CARAVANS OF MERCHANTS AND ARMIES. AFTER THE ROMAN CONQUEST THINGS CHANGED.

ROADS WHICH WERE BETTER AND A BIT SAFER BENEFITED THE FLOOD OF PILGRIMS GOING TO JERUSALEM FOR THE GREAT FESTIVALS AND ALSO THE FIRST CHRISTIANS TAKING THE 'GOOD NEWS' TO PAGAN PEOPLE.

THE ROMAN ROADS

Pont du Gard

aqueduct with three levels

How roads were built

PAVING MADE OF LARGE BASALT STONES

GUTTER

SAND AND GRAVEL

PEBBLES

STONES

MILESTONE PLACED EVERY 1000 PACES

TO ANTIOCH

DAMASCUS

Capernaum

Tiberias

Nazareth

Caesarea

WAY OF THE SEA

Samaria

Emmaus

Jerusalem

Bethlehem

Jericho

ROYAL ROAD

DRESS FOR TRAVEL

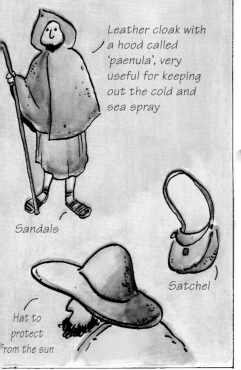

Leather cloak with a hood called 'paenula', very useful for keeping out the cold and sea spray

Sandals

Satchel

Hat to protect from the sun

DIFFERENT TYPES OF CART

TWO-WHEELED CART FOR SHORT TRIPS

MULES AND OXEN

FOUR-WHEELED CART FOR LONG JOURNEYS

HORSES

WHERE CAN WE SPEND THE NIGHT?

IN THE INN OR 'CARAVANSERAI', WHERE IT WAS ALSO POSSIBLE TO STABLE THE ANIMALS AND GIVE THEM DRINK. OTHER SERVICES (FOOD, FODDER, ETC.) COST EXTRA.

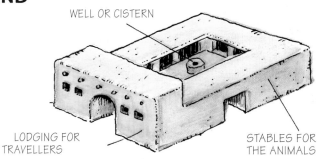

WELL OR CISTERN

LODGING FOR TRAVELLERS

STABLES FOR THE ANIMALS

MANY TRAVELLED ON FOOT. FOR SAFETY'S SAKE THEY TRAVELLED IN SMALL GROUPS.

LAMENT OF A TRAVELLER:

'I HAVE BEEN SHIPWRECKED THREE TIMES AND SPENT TWENTY-FOUR HOURS LOST AT SEA.'
AND AGAIN: 'OFTEN ON FOOT BY ROAD AND WITH DANGER FROM RIVERS, DANGER FROM ROBBERS' (II CORINTHIANS 11. 25B–26A)
THE PERSON SPEAKING IS THE APOSTLE PAUL, WHO INDEFATIGABLY COVERED MILE AFTER MILE.

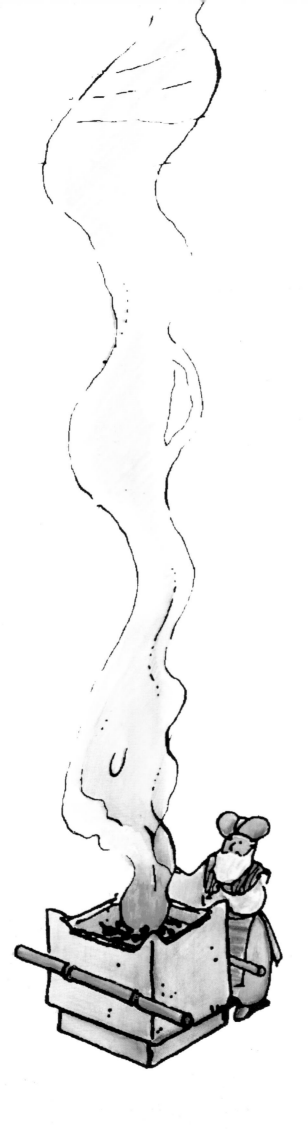

FAITH
AND RELIGIOUS LIFE

THE SABBATH

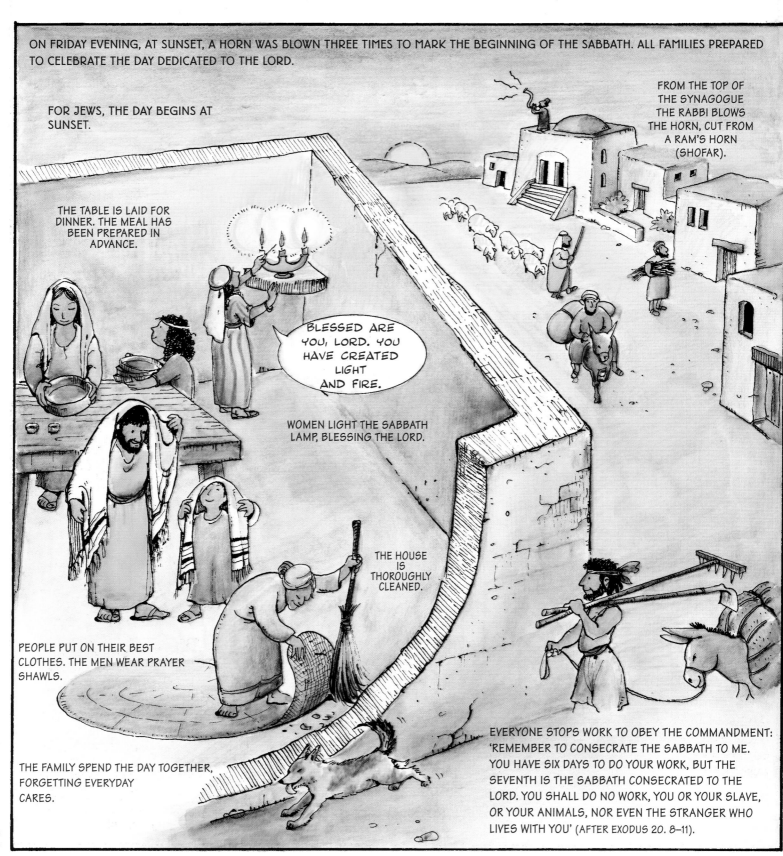

ON FRIDAY EVENING, AT SUNSET, A HORN WAS BLOWN THREE TIMES TO MARK THE BEGINNING OF THE SABBATH. ALL FAMILIES PREPARED TO CELEBRATE THE DAY DEDICATED TO THE LORD.

FOR JEWS, THE DAY BEGINS AT SUNSET.

FROM THE TOP OF THE SYNAGOGUE THE RABBI BLOWS THE HORN, CUT FROM A RAM'S HORN (SHOFAR).

THE TABLE IS LAID FOR DINNER. THE MEAL HAS BEEN PREPARED IN ADVANCE.

BLESSED ARE YOU, LORD. YOU HAVE CREATED LIGHT AND FIRE.

WOMEN LIGHT THE SABBATH LAMP, BLESSING THE LORD.

THE HOUSE IS THOROUGHLY CLEANED.

PEOPLE PUT ON THEIR BEST CLOTHES. THE MEN WEAR PRAYER SHAWLS.

THE FAMILY SPEND THE DAY TOGETHER, FORGETTING EVERYDAY CARES.

EVERYONE STOPS WORK TO OBEY THE COMMANDMENT: 'REMEMBER TO CONSECRATE THE SABBATH TO ME. YOU HAVE SIX DAYS TO DO YOUR WORK, BUT THE SEVENTH IS THE SABBATH CONSECRATED TO THE LORD. YOU SHALL DO NO WORK, YOU OR YOUR SLAVE, OR YOUR ANIMALS, NOR EVEN THE STRANGER WHO LIVES WITH YOU' (AFTER EXODUS 20. 8–11).

THE SABBATH EVENING MEAL

THE HEAD OF THE FAMILY BLESSES THE SABBATH BY RAISING A CUP OF WINE. DURING THE MEAL, SONGS ARE SUNG AND PRAYERS RECITED.

ON THE TABLE, AMONG THE DIFFERENT DISHES ARE ALWAYS TWO WHOLE LOAVES AND WINE.

THE CELEBRATION IN THE SYNAGOGUE IS ANOTHER IMPORTANT MOMENT OF THE SABBATH.

SO GREAT IS THE SABBATH JOY THAT PEOPLE TRY TO PROLONG THE DAY BY DINING LATER. THE MOMENT THE FIRST THREE STARS APPEAR IN THE SKY THE SABBATH ENDS. THE FAMILY CELEBRATES THE END OF THE SABBATH BY ASKING THE LORD TO BLESS THE WORK OF THE NEW WEEK.

SCRUPULOUS OBSERVANCE OF THE SABBATH COULD CAUSE PROBLEMS, INCLUDING FINANCIAL PROBLEMS, SO SOME PEOPLE WORKED IN SECRET. TO ENCOURAGE EVERYONE NOT TO WORK AND TO UNIFY THE RITES, OVER THE CENTURIES RULES AND REGULATIONS WERE FIXED WHICH SCHOLARS DEBATED, SOMETIMES VIGOROUSLY.

EVEN JESUS, WHO ALWAYS CELEBRATED THE SABBATH WITH HIS DISCIPLES, JOINED IN THE DEBATE. HE GAVE THE SABBATH A PROFOUND MEANING:

'THE SABBATH WAS MADE FOR MAN AND NOT MAN FOR THE SABBATH' (MARK 2. 27).

HOW DID THE SABBATH COME INTO BEING ?

AMONG ALL PEOPLES THERE ARE FESTIVALS LINKED TO THE CYCLE OF NATURE. WHAT IS NEW AMONG THE JEWS BY COMPARISON WITH NEIGHBORING PEOPLES IS THAT THEY OBSERVE ONE DAY OF REST EACH WEEK. THEY CALL IT THE **SABBATH** AND CONSECRATE IT TO THE LORD (GENESIS 2. 2–3). WHEN THERE IS A LOT OF WORK, A DAY OF REST RELIEVES BOTH MEN AND ANIMALS.

FESTIVAL OF THE GRAPE HARVEST

HARVEST FESTIVAL

WHEN THE JEWS WERE EXILED IN **BABYLON** THEY NO LONGER HAD THE TEMPLE, SO RESPECTING THE SABBATH WAS VERY IMPORTANT. MOREOVER, TO HAVE A DAY OF REST IN THE MIDST OF DIFFERENT PEOPLES BECAME A DISTINGUISHING MARK.

PRAYER

THE GOSPELS TELL US THAT JESUS OFTEN PRAYED:

... JESUS WENT UP A MOUNTAIN AND PRAYED TO GOD ALL NIGHT. WHEN DAY BROKE, HE TOOK A DECISION: GATHERING TOGETHER THE DISCIPLES, HE CHOSE TWELVE AND CALLED THEM APOSTLES, SINCE THEY WERE SENT TO PROCLAIM THE GOOD NEWS (AFTER LUKE 6. 12–13).

JESUS TOOK FIVE LOAVES AND TWO FISHES. HE RAISED HIS EYES TO HEAVEN AND SPOKE THE BLESSING. THEN HE BEGAN TO SHARE THE BREAD AND GAVE IT TO THE DISCIPLES FOR THEM TO DISTRIBUTE (MARK 6. 41–42).

'WHEN YOU PRAY, DO NOT GO ON AND ON . . . FOR YOUR FATHER KNOWS WHAT YOU NEED EVEN BEFORE YOU ASK. SO PRAY LIKE THIS: OUR FATHER WHO ART IN HEAVEN . . .' (MATTHEW 6. 7–9).

JESUS LEARNED TO PRAY IN HIS YOUTH

FOR ALL THE FAMILY, PRAYER WAS PART OF LIFE AND GAVE IT A MEANING DAY AFTER DAY, WHETHER IN JOY OR SORROW.

THE FINEST COLLECTION OF PRAYERS IS IN THE BOOK OF PSALMS. THERE ARE PRAYERS FOR ALL TIMES AND ALL SITUATIONS.

MORNING PRAYER

I TURN TO YOU, LORD. IN THE MORNING YOU HEAR MY VOICE. IN THE MORNING I PREPARE FOR YOU AND REMAIN AWAKE (PSALM 5).

EVENING PRAYER

I LIE DOWN AND GO TO SLEEP IN PEACE, FOR YOU ALONE, LORD, MAKE ME DWELL IN SAFETY (PSALM 4).

THE PEOPLE OF JESUS

SPEAKING TO GOD IS AN IMPORTANT AND SERIOUS MATTER. ADOLESCENTS AND ADULTS COVER THEIR HEADS AND SHOULDERS WITH A SPECIAL SHAWL (TALLIT) AND PUT A LITTLE BOX (TEPHILLAH) ON THEIR ARMS AND FOREHEADS. THIS CONTAINS PARCHMENT SCROLLS ON WHICH ARE WRITTEN DEUTERONOMY 6. 4-9 AND 11. 13-21.

THE FAMILY

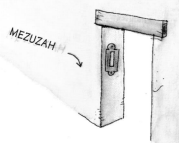

MEZUZAH

A SIMILAR BOX CONTAINING THE SAME VERSES IS FIXED ON THE DOORPOST.

IN THE TEMPLE AND THE SYNAGOGUE

IN THE JERUSALEM TEMPLE AND IN THE SYNAGOGUES THE MOST IMPORTANT PRAYER IS THE 'SHEMA ISRAEL', WHICH MEANS 'HEAR, ISRAEL'. IT QUOTES DEUTERONOMY 6. 4-9.

HEAR, ISRAEL, THE LORD IS OUR GOD, THE LORD IS ONE.

I WILL PRAISE THE NAME OF THE LORD WITH A SONG. I WILL MAGNIFY HIM WITH THANKSGIVING. THIS WILL PLEASE THE LORD MORE THAN AN OX, OR A BULL WITH HORNS AND HOOFS.

(PSALM 69. 31-32)

... IN ANCIENT TIMES

THOSE WHO PRAY ADDRESS THE GOD OF ABRAHAM, ISAAC AND JACOB, THE LORD WHO HAS ALWAYS BEEN PRESENT IN ISRAEL AS IN THE TIME OF KING DAVID, SAMUEL AND MOSES.

THE PRAYER OF DAVID

WHO AM I LORD GOD ... THAT YOU HAVE BROUGHT ME THIS FAR? AND WHAT MORE COULD I SAY, SINCE YOU KNOW YOUR SERVANT, LORD GOD?
(II SAMUEL 7. 18-20).

THE PRAYER OF HANNAH
SAMUEL'S MOTHER

MY SOUL EXULTS IN THE LORD,
MY STRENGTH IS EXALTED FOR THE LORD;
MY MOUTH DERIDES MY RIVALS ...
YES, I EXULT IN YOUR SALVATION
(I SAMUEL 2. 1).

THE PRAYER OF MOSES

THIS PEOPLE HAS COMMITTED GREAT SIN. THEY HAVE MADE FOR THEMSELVES GODS OF GOLD. IF YOU WILL, FORGIVE THEIR SIN - IF NOT, BLOT ME FROM YOUR BOOK
(EXODUS 32. 31-32).

 THERE ARE SEVEN JEWISH FESTIVALS ...

 ... PLUS THE CHRISTIAN CHRISTMAS AND EASTER ...

... THAT MAKES NINE

 HOW I LIKE INTERFAITH DIALOGUE

THE FESTIVALS IN ISRAEL

For the Jews the year begins in . . .

FOR THE JEWISH PEOPLE, TIME WAS MARKED BY IMPORTANT FESTIVALS: MOMENTS OF JOY AND RECOLLECTION, SPECIAL DAYS FOR EXPRESSING ONE'S RECOGNITION AND PRAISE OF THE LORD AND ALSO FOR MAKING A SOLEMN PLEDGE TO RENEW ONE'S LIFE.

September

ROSH HA-SHANAH
NEW YEAR'S DAY

 IT RECALLS THE CREATION OF THE WORLD. THE SOUND OF THE HORN (SHOPHAR) INVITES EVERYONE TO REFLECT ON THEIR LIVES AND REPENT.

YOM KIPPUR
THE DAY OF ATONEMENT

THE PEOPLE ASK FORGIVENESS FOR ALL THEIR SINS. A GOAT IS SYMBOLICALLY LOADED WITH ALL THESE SINS AND DRIVEN INTO THE WILDERNESS.

September–October

SUCCOTH
FEAST OF BOOTHS

May–June

SHABUOT
PENTECOST

March–April

PESACH
PASSOVER

 February

THE BOOK OF ESTHER IS READ AND PRESENTS ARE EXCHANGED.

PURIM
FESTIVAL OF JOY (OR OF LOTS)

November–December

HANUKKAH
FEAST OF LIGHT

IT COMMEMORATES THE CLEANSING OF THE TEMPLE PROFANED BY THE SYRIANS.

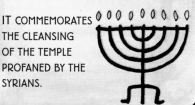

46

THREE TIMES A YEAR EVERY ISRAELITE HAD TO GO ON FOOT TO THE TEMPLE IN JERUSALEM (EXODUS 23. 14). PEOPLE WENT JOYFULLY IN GROUPS TO THE HOLY CITY WHICH WELCOMED THEM WITH LIGHT, SINGING AND DANCING IN HONOR OF THE LORD WHO FREES HIS PEOPLE FROM SLAVERY. AFTER THE DESTRUCTION OF THE TEMPLE IN AD 70, THE CELEBRATION TOOK PLACE AT HOME AMONG THE FAMILY.

THE PILGRIMAGE FESTIVALS

PESACH
PASSOVER

IT IS CELEBRATED IN MARCH OR APRIL AND LASTS A WEEK.

THE FESTIVAL RECALLS THE LIBERATION FROM SLAVERY IN EGYPT AND COMMEMORATES THE BEGINNING OF SPRING.

PILGRIMS GO TO THE TEMPLE, WHERE THEY OFFER A LAMB AS SACRIFICE WITH UNLEAVENED BREAD AND THE FIRST FRUITS OF THE EARTH.

GROUPS OF PILGRIMS MEET FOR THE PASSOVER MEAL. THE BOOK OF EXODUS IS READ.

SHABUOT
PENTECOST

THIS FESTIVAL IS CELEBRATED IN MAY OR JUNE AND LASTS TWO WEEKS.

IT RECALLS THE GIFT OF THE LAW. AT THE SAME TIME THE PEOPLE GIVE THANKS FOR THE HARVEST.

THE PILGRIMS ENTER THE TEMPLE SINGING AND OFFER THE FIRST FRUITS OF THE HARVEST ALONG WITH TWO LEAVENED LOAVES MADE OF NEW FLOUR.

SUCCOTH
FEAST OF BOOTHS

IT IS CELEBRATED IN SEPTEMBER OR OCTOBER AND LASTS EIGHT DAYS.

IT RECALLS THE TIME IN THE WILDERNESS AFTER THE EXODUS FROM EGYPT WHEN THE PEOPLE HAD TO BUILD TEMPORARY DWELLINGS. DURING THIS FESTIVAL PEOPLE ALSO THANKED GOD FOR THE END OF THE HARVEST AND GRAPE HARVEST.

PEOPLE LIVE IN THE OPEN AIR IN CABINS MADE WITH BRANCHES OF TREES. THERE IS SINGING AND DANCING.

THE BOOTH IS ALSO THE SYMBOL OF HUMAN FRAGILITY AND IMPERFECTION. THE ROOF IS MADE OF BRANCHES, LEAVES AND FLOWERS SO AS TO LET IN RAYS OF SUN, STARLIGHT AND DROPS OF RAIN.

HOW HUNGRY I AM!
CLASSICAL QUESTION:

WHAT'S TO EAT?

SOUP!

GLURP

CLASSICAL REPLY

THE PASSOVER MEAL

THE DAY BEFORE PASSOVER IN A HOUSE IN JERUSALEM . . .

GET UP, CHILDREN! WE'VE LOTS TO DO TODAY.

LOOK IN ALL THE CORNERS AND MAKE SURE THAT NOT A SPOT OF LEAVENED BREAD IS THERE.

WHY DO WE BURN IT NOW?

WE'RE GETTING RID OF THE OLD LEAVEN IN OUR HOUSE. WE MUST ALSO SEARCH OUR HEARTS SO SOMETHING NEW CAN ENTER THEM.

ON PASSOVER MORNING A LAMB IS TAKEN TO THE TEMPLE FOR THE PRIEST TO OFFER AS A SACRIFICE.

SHALOM, PILGRIM! ARE YOU ALONE THIS EVENING? COME AND CELEBRATE THE PASSOVER WITH ME.

SHALOM! THANK YOU, I'LL BE THERE

THEN THE LAMB IS ROASTED AT HOME.

IT IS EVENING. IN THE FAMILY ALL PUT ON THEIR BEST CLOTHES TO CELEBRATE **PASSOVER**.

SIT COMFORTABLY, FOR THE LORD HAS GIVEN US REST.

WHAT IS IN THE DISH?

ROAST LAMB IN MEMORY OF WHAT OUR FATHERS ATE AT THE EXODUS FROM EGYPT ...

... AND BITTER HERBS, FOR THE SLAVERY WAS VERY HARSH.

THERE ARE ALSO THREE LOAVES OF UNLEAVENED BREAD, AS OUR FATHERS LEFT IN GREAT HASTE AND DID NOT HAVE TIME TO LET THE DOUGH RISE.

AND SALT WATER IN MEMORY OF TEARS SHED.

WHAT ABOUT THIS BROWN SAUCE?

IT RECALLS THE STRAW AND CLAY WITH WHICH OUR FATHERS MADE BRICKS FOR THE EGYPTIANS.

THIS EVENING WE THANK GOD. DRINKING THIS CUP OF WINE, WE TRANSFORM OUR SADNESS INTO JOY.

BENJAMIN IS THE YOUNGEST MEMBER OF THE FAMILY. HE MUST ASK THE RITUAL QUESTION.

GO TO IT, BEN!

WHY IS THIS NIGHT DIFFERENT FROM ALL OTHER NIGHTS?

BECAUSE WE WERE SLAVES OF THE PHARAOH OF EGYPT ...

... AND THE LORD FREED FROM SLAVERY NOT ONLY OUR FATHERS BUT EACH ONE OF US.

HURRAH!

PRAISE THE LORD, ALL PEOPLES; CELEBRATE HIM, ALL LANDS! HE HAS SHOWN HIS GREAT LOVE FOR US. THE LORD IS FAITHFUL FOR EVER (PSALM 117).

THE SANCTUARY, THE TENT, THE ARK

THE BIBLE OFTEN MENTIONS **MEMORIAL STONES** OR **STONES OF WITNESS**, SET UP WHERE THE PATRIARCHS AND JUDGES HAD EXPERIENCED THE PRESENCE OF THE LORD IN A SPECIAL PLACE AT A SPECIFIC TIME (GENESIS 12. 6-7; 28. 10-22; 33. 18-20; JOSHUA 4. 6-9; 24. 26-27). THESE PLACES WERE DECLARED HOLY AND CALLED '**HIGH PLACES**' OR '**SANCTUARIES**'. THAT DID NOT MEAN THAT GOD LIVED THERE BUT THAT HE HAD SHOWN HIMSELF THERE. FAMILIES WENT THERE OFTEN. THE **MEMORY OF THE PAST** AND GOD'S **PROMISES** FOR THE **FUTURE** GAVE LIGHT AND STRENGTH FOR COPING WITH THE **PRESENT**.

SOMETIMES A TEMPLE WAS BUILT IN THE SANCTUARY. SANCTUARIES WERE THE CENTER OF THE RELIGIOUS AND CIVIL LIFE OF ISRAEL. SACRIFICES AND FESTIVALS WERE CELEBRATED THERE, PRIESTS TAUGHT THE LAW AND KINGS WERE CONSECRATED.

IN CANAAN BEFORE THE ARRIVAL OF THE ISRAELITES, OTHER PEOPLES WORSHIPPED THEIR GODS IN SANCTUARIES. ISRAEL WAS STRONGLY TEMPTED TO ADOPT THE LOCAL RITES AND IDENTIFY THE LORD WITH THE CANAANITE IDOLS. THE **PROPHETS** WARNED AGAINST THIS DANGER. LITTLE BY LITTLE THE 'HIGH PLACES' WERE SUPPRESSED AND THE **JERUSALEM TEMPLE** WAS CONSIDERED ISRAEL'S SOLE SANCTUARY.

THE TENT OF MEETING

NOMADS LIVE IN TENTS. IN THE WILDERNESS, AFTER THEIR EXODUS FROM EGYPT, THE ISRAELITES LIVED IN TENTS. IN THE MIDDLE OF THE CAMP THEY SET UP A SPECIAL TENT. THIS WAS THE **TABERNACLE**, A MOBILE SANCTUARY WHERE THE PEOPLE MET THE LORD. SO THE TABERNACLE IS ALSO CALLED THE **TENT OF MEETING**.

THE ARK

THE **ARK** WAS KEPT IN THE TABERNACLE. THE BOOK OF EXODUS DESCRIBES THE ARK AS A PORTABLE BOX OF ACACIA WOOD COVERED WITH GOLD AND MADE TO CONTAIN THE **TABLETS OF THE LAW**. THE ARK WENT WITH THE PEOPLE IN THE WILDERNESS AND TO WAR (JOSHUA 6. 11–13; I SAMUEL 4–6). LATER, KING DAVID HAD THE ARK BROUGHT TO JERUSALEM.

51

WHO DECIDES WHAT IS RIGHT AND WHAT IS WRONG?

AT SCHOOL IT'S MY TEACHER ...

AT HOME IT'S MY PARENTS ...

... MY PROBLEM IS IN THE BUS!

LAW AND JUSTICE

FOR ISRAEL, **GOD** WAS ALWAYS THE SOURCE OF JUSTICE AND LAW. THE **RULES OF LIFE** WERE TO BE FOUND IN THE BIBLE. THEY WERE ABOUT WORSHIP AND LIVING IN COMMUNITY. ISRAEL COULD NOT BEHAVE LIKE PAGAN PEOPLES. IT HAD TO LEARN TO WORSHIP ONE GOD.

WORSHIP OF GOD WAS EXPRESSED NOT ONLY IN THE CULT BUT ALSO IN LIFE WITH OTHERS. THIS LIFE HAD TO BE INSPIRED BY THE RULES OF THE COVENANT BETWEEN GOD AND HIS PEOPLE, LIKE **RESPECT**, **LOVE** AND **JUSTICE**.

DEBORAH, PROPHETESS AND JUDGE, HEARS A COMPLAINT.

THE KING AND THE LAW: A COMPARISON

IN MESOPOTAMIA

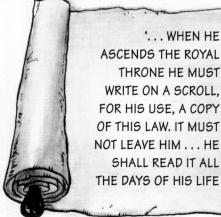

'I, HAMMURABI, AM THE KING OF JUSTICE TO WHOM SHAMASH HAS ENTRUSTED THE LAW. NOTHING IS BETTER THAN MY WORDS, NOTHING EQUALS MY ACTS, ONLY FOOLS WILL IGNORE THEM ...'
(CODE OF HAMMURABI)

IN ISRAEL

'... WHEN HE ASCENDS THE ROYAL THRONE HE MUST WRITE ON A SCROLL, FOR HIS USE, A COPY OF THIS LAW. IT MUST NOT LEAVE HIM ... HE SHALL READ IT ALL THE DAYS OF HIS LIFE TO LEARN TO RESPECT YAHWEH HIS GOD BY OBSERVING ALL THE WORDS OF THIS LAW ... IN THIS WAY HE WILL AVOID LORDING IT OVER HIS BROTHERS ...'
(AFTER DEUTERONOMY 17. 18–20)

WHO ADMINISTERS JUSTICE?

AS A RULE, JUSTICE WAS ADMINISTERED BY THE **ELDERS**, SITTING NEAR THE GATE OF THE TOWN (RUTH 4. 1–2). THEY EXAMINED CASES SUBMITTED TO THEM. COMPLICATED CASES WERE REFERRED TO THE **PRIESTS** AT THE SANCTUARIES OR TO FAMOUS **JUDGES** LIKE DEBORAH (SEE THE PICTURE OPPOSITE) (JUDGES 4.4–5).
LATER, IN SOME CASES AN APPEAL COULD BE MADE TO THE **KING** (I KINGS 3.16–28).

THREE GOLDEN RULES
for justice in Israel

✧ YOU SHALL NOT TAKE A BRIBE, FOR A BRIBE BLINDS THE EYES OF THE WISE AND PERVERTS THE CAUSE OF THE RIGHTEOUS (DEUTERONOMY 16. 20).

✧ PUNISHMENT MUST NOT BE TOO STRICT (DEUTERONOMY 25. 1–3).

✧ THE TESTIMONY OF A SINGLE WITNESS SHALL NOT SUFFICE. THE ACCUSATION MUST BE MADE BY TWO OR THREE WITNESSES (DEUTERONOMY 19. 15).

THE LAW PROTECTS THE WEAKEST

PART OF THE **HARVEST** (GRAIN, OLIVES, GRAPES) WAS LEFT IN THE FIELDS, SO THAT THE POOR AND STRANGERS COULD GATHER IT (DEUTERONOMY 24. 19–22).

IF A POOR MAN'S **CLOAK** WAS TAKEN IN PLEDGE, IT HAD TO BE RETURNED TO HIM BY SUNSET SO HE COULD COVER HIMSELF WITH IT AT NIGHT (DEUTERONOMY 24. 12–16).

NOT the millstone!

THE **MILLSTONE** OF THE HOUSE CANNOT BE TAKEN AS A PLEDGE AS IT IS NECESSARY FOR EVERYDAY LIFE (DEUTERONOMY 24. 6).

... EVEN ANIMALS!

'YOU SHALL NOT **MUZZLE** THE OX WHICH TREADS THE GRAIN' (DEUTERONOMY 25. 4).

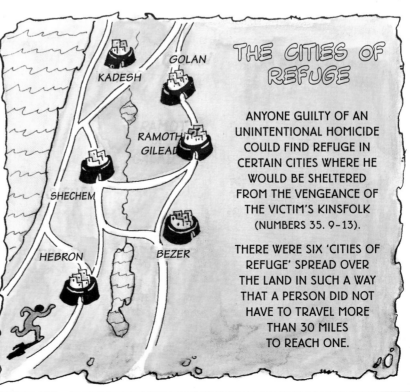

THE CITIES OF REFUGE

ANYONE GUILTY OF AN UNINTENTIONAL HOMICIDE COULD FIND REFUGE IN CERTAIN CITIES WHERE HE WOULD BE SHELTERED FROM THE VENGEANCE OF THE VICTIM'S KINSFOLK (NUMBERS 35. 9–13).

THERE WERE SIX 'CITIES OF REFUGE' SPREAD OVER THE LAND IN SUCH A WAY THAT A PERSON DID NOT HAVE TO TRAVEL MORE THAN 30 MILES TO REACH ONE.

GOLAN
KADESH
RAMOTH GILEAD
SHECHEM
HEBRON
BEZER

WHAT HAVE YOU DONE WELL?

A THANKSGIVING SACRIFICE. I GOT 'GOOD' IN DICTATION!

SACRIFICES IN THE OLD TESTAMENT

IN THE ANCIENT WORLD

SACRIFICES ARE AN IMPORTANT ELEMENT OF ALL ANCIENT RELIGIONS. SACRIFICE IS AN ACT PERFORMED IN HONOR OF THE DEITY. IT CONSISTS IN KILLING AN **ANIMAL** OR OFFERING THE **FRUITS OF THE EARTH** OR **PERFUMES**.

IN EGYPT

IN MESOPOTAMIA

IN ROME

IN VERY ANCIENT TIMES, **HUMAN** VICTIMS WERE ALSO OFFERED. BY TELLING THE STORY OF THE SACRIFICE OF ISAAC, THE AUTHORS OF GENESIS SEEK TO MAKE US UNDERSTAND THAT GOD DOES NOT WANT HUMAN SACRIFICES (GENESIS 22. 1–19).

ALTARS

THE ALTAR IS THE PLACE OF SACRIFICE. THE BIBLE TELLS US OF ALTARS MADE OF PILED-UP **EARTH** OR **STONES** BUT THERE IS NO TRACE OF ANY OF THESE.

WHEN PEOPLE WERE STILL NOMADIC, ALTARS LIKE THIS WERE BUILT TO MARK A PARTICULARLY IMPORTANT PLACE FOR THE FAMILY OR CLAN (GENESIS 12. 7). SACRIFICES WERE OFFERED BY THE **HEAD OF THE FAMILY** OR THE **CHIEF OF THE CLAN**. IN ISRAEL, ARCHAEOLOGISTS HAVE FOUND EXTREMELY ANCIENT **STONE** ALTARS.

OVER TIME, JERUSALEM BECAME THE RELIGIOUS CENTER OF ISRAEL. SACRIFICES WERE OFFERED ONLY IN THE **TEMPLE** WITH **PRIESTS**. THE TEMPLE ALTAR WAS BRONZE. IT WAS MORE THAN 30 FEET LONG AND 15 FEET HIGH. PRIESTS AND ANIMALS WENT UP TO IT BY A STAIRCASE.

SACRIFICES AS GIFTS

IN THE ANCIENT WORLD, GIFTS WERE VERY IMPORTANT IN PERSONAL RELATIONS.

FOR THE MEN AND WOMEN OF THE BIBLE, EVERY GOOD THING IS A **GIFT FROM GOD** WHICH MUST BE RESPONDED TO WITH A PERSONAL OFFERING.

AT HARVEST TIME THE FIRST FRUITS OF THE EARTH WERE OFFERED TO THE LORD.

AFTER GIVING BIRTH, EVERY WOMAN MADE AN OFFERING TO THE LORD. IF THE WOMAN WAS POOR, THE OFFERING COULD BE MODEST. PEOPLE CURED OF SERIOUS ILLNESSES ALSO OFFERED SACRIFICES TO GOD.

SACRIFICES AS PRAYER

FOR THE PEOPLE OF ISRAEL, SACRIFICES WERE A FORM OF PRAYER EXPRESSED IN ACTIONS RATHER THAN WORDS. IN PRAYER WE CAN THANK THE LORD, ASK HIS FORGIVENESS OR SIMPLY FEEL CLOSE TO HIM. SIMILARLY, IN OLD TESTAMENT TIMES SACRIFICES WERE **THANKSGIVING**, A REQUEST FOR **FORGIVENESS** OR A MOMENT OF **COMMUNION** WITH THE LORD.

WHEN THE JERUSALEM TEMPLE WAS DESTROYED BY THE ROMANS, SACRIFICES WERE ABOLISHED. SO THE UTMOST IMPORTANCE WAS ATTACHED TO THE **READING** AND **TEACHING** OF **SCRIPTURE** AND **PRAYER**.

BUT THINGS WERE NOT ALWAYS LIKE THAT. MANY **PROPHETS WARNED** AGAINST SEEING SACRIFICE AS AN ALMOST MAGICAL RITE TO MAKE GOD DO WHAT THEY WANTED, THUS IGNORING RESPECT FOR THE LAW AND REPENTANCE OF SIN (AMOS 5. 21-42).

THE PSALMS AND MUSIC

THE **PSALMS** ARE POETIC COMPOSITIONS WHICH CAN BE COMPARED WITH OUR HYMNS. SEVERAL PSALMS ARE ATTRIBUTED TO DAVID, BUT IT IS NOT CERTAIN THAT HE WROTE THEM. NOT EVERY PSALM CAN BE DATED PRECISELY, BUT WE CAN BE SURE THAT SOME PSALMS ARE VERY OLD AND GO BACK TO THE TIME OF THE KINGS. OTHERS WERE COMPOSED DURING THE EXILE IN BABYLON AND YET OTHERS AFTER THE RETURN OF THE EXILES TO ISRAEL.

A CRY OF ANGUISH

My God, my God,
why have you forsaken me?
Salvation is far from me,
from the words that I groan.

But you are holy,
enthroned on the praise of Israel.
Our fathers trusted in you,
they hoped and you delivered them.
When they cried to you they were saved;
in you they hoped and were not
disappointed.

All those who see me mock at me,
they snigger and shake their heads.
Lord be not far from me.
O my strength, come quickly to my help.

(Psalm 22)

A LAMENTATION AFTER THE DESTRUCTION OF THE TEMPLE

Turn your steps towards these perpetual ruins;
the enemy has destroyed everything in the sanctuary.
We saw them swing the axe
as deep in the forest
when they broke the doors
with hammers and hatchets.
They set your sanctuary on fire,
desecrated and razed the dwelling place of your name.
No one sees our signs;
there are no longer any prophets.
How long will it be?
No one among us knows.
How long, O God, will the enemy blaspheme?
Will he ever stop scorning your name?

(Psalm 74)

A SONG OF TRUST

The Lord is my shepherd:
I shall lack nothing.
He will make me lie down
in green pastures
and lead me to quiet waters.
He will revive me.
He leads me by the right way
for the honour of his name.

(Psalm 23)

FROM TEARS TO JOY

When the Lord brought back the captives to Zion,
we were as in a dream.
Then our mouth was filled with laughter,
and our tongue with shouts of joy.
Then they said among the nations,
'The Lord has done marvels for us.'
The Lord has done great things for us.
We are glad.
Restore our fortunes, Lord,
like the rivers of the desert.

(Psalm 126)

THESE SONGS ARE CALLED 'PSALMS'. THIS WORD IS GREEK IN ORIGIN AND DENOTES A POEM WRITTEN TO BE ACCOMPANIED BY A MUSICAL INSTRUMENT. THE PSALMS EXPRESS THE FEELING OF THE BELIEVER AND THE PRAYER OF THE PEOPLE OF ISRAEL, ITS DOUBTS AND ITS JOY, ITS DESPAIR AND ITS TRUST. THERE IS A GROUP OF PSALMS FOR EACH PERIOD OF THE HISTORY OF ISRAEL.

MUSIC

THE JEWS LOVED SINGING AND MUSIC. EVERY EVENT – BIRTHS, MARRIAGES, DEATHS, CORONATIONS, RELIGIOUS FESTIVALS – WAS ACCOMPANIED BY INSTRUMENTAL MUSIC, AN ORCHESTRA AND A CHOIR. ARCHAEOLOGY HELPS US TO RECONSTRUCT THE INSTRUMENTS BUT WE KNOW NOTHING OF THE MUSIC OF THE TIME. NEVERTHELESS, THE TYPE OF INSTRUMENTS RECONSTRUCTED TELLS US THAT THE MUSIC WAS ABOVE ALL RHYTHMIC AND SERVED TO ACCOMPANY SUNG AND RECITED TEXTS AND DANCES.

WIND INSTRUMENTS
TRUMPET
FLUTE

STRINGED INSTRUMENTS
LYRE
HARP
ZITHER

PERCUSSION
DRUMS
TYMPANI
CYMBALS
BELLS

Praise the Lord, he is good!

His love for us is eternal

THE BIBLE TELLS US THAT MUSIC WAS SO IMPORTANT FOR DAVID THAT HE ORDERED 4,000 SINGERS TO PRAISE THE LORD ACCOMPANIED BY MUSICAL INSTRUMENTS WHICH HE HIMSELF HAD SPECIFIED (I CHRONICLES 23. 5 AND 25. 1-9). WITH ITS 120 SILVER TRUMPETS PLAYED BY PRIESTS, THE MUSIC OF THE TEMPLE WAS IMPRESSIVE (II CHRONICLES 5. 12-13).

DANCING

THERE WAS SINGING AND DANCING AT ALL THE FESTIVALS. PEOPLE ALSO DANCED TO CELEBRATE A VICTORY OR AT HARVEST FESTIVALS. THE JEWS WERE A HAPPY PEOPLE WHO EVEN DANCED DURING CELEBRATIONS (II SAMUEL 6. 5). PROBABLY MEN AND WOMEN DANCED SEPARATELY.

HEROD'S TEMPLE

JERUSALEM WAS DOMINATED BY THE IMPOSING MARBLE BUILDING OF
THE TEMPLE. IT WAS VERY RICHLY DECORATED WITH GOLD AND
COPPER AND ITS WALLS SHONE IN THE SUN.
THE TEMPLE WAS REBUILT IN THIS SPLENDOUR BY
HEROD, STARTING IN 19 BC, AND REQUIRED
MORE THAN 10,000 WORKMEN.

IN THE TIME OF JESUS, WORK ON THE TEMPLE WAS WELL
ADVANCED. IT WOULD BE FINISHED IN 64, 6 YEARS BEFORE
ITS DESTRUCTION BY THE ROMANS IN 70. ALL THAT IS LEFT IS
THE VAST TERRACE. ITS WEST SIDE IS CALLED THE 'WAILING
WALL'. JEWS STILL GO THERE TODAY TO LAMENT THE
DESTRUCTION OF THE TEMPLE.

Royal portico

Entrance from the
upper city

Court of the
Gentiles

Entrance from
the lower city

Rabbis
teaching

Money
changers

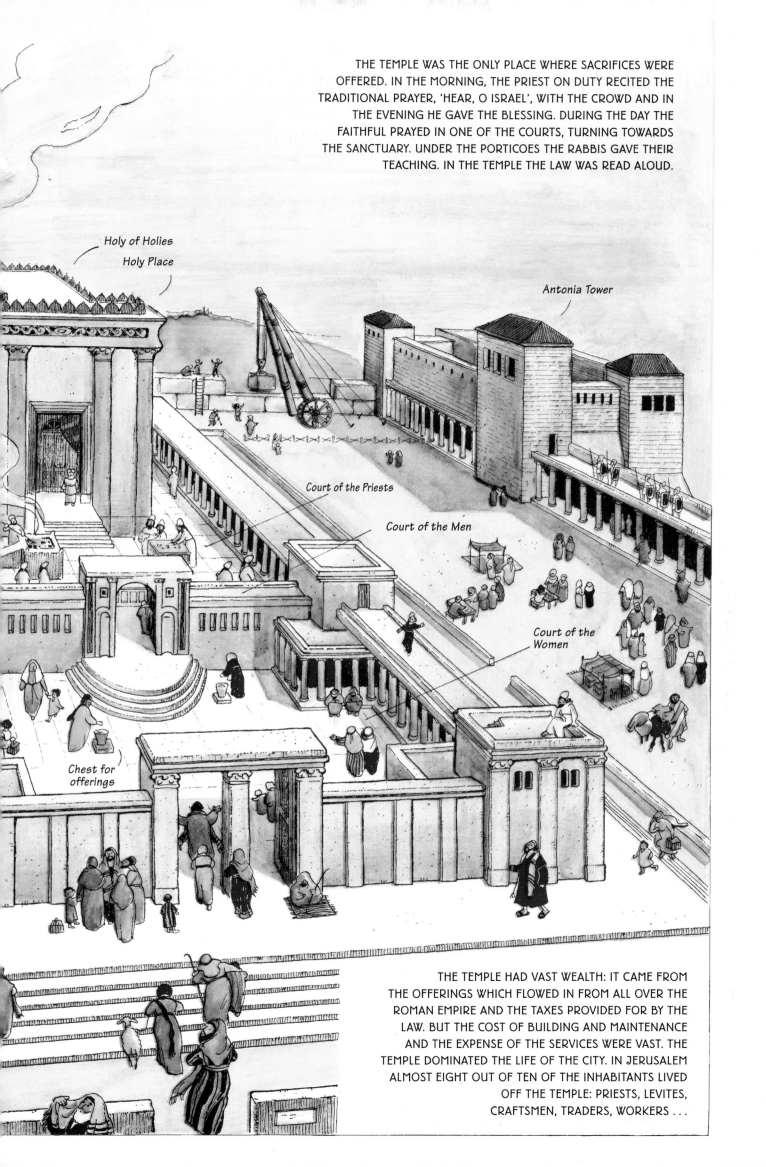

THE TEMPLE WAS THE ONLY PLACE WHERE SACRIFICES WERE OFFERED. IN THE MORNING, THE PRIEST ON DUTY RECITED THE TRADITIONAL PRAYER, 'HEAR, O ISRAEL', WITH THE CROWD AND IN THE EVENING HE GAVE THE BLESSING. DURING THE DAY THE FAITHFUL PRAYED IN ONE OF THE COURTS, TURNING TOWARDS THE SANCTUARY. UNDER THE PORTICOES THE RABBIS GAVE THEIR TEACHING. IN THE TEMPLE THE LAW WAS READ ALOUD.

Holy of Holies

Holy Place

Antonia Tower

Court of the Priests

Court of the Men

Court of the Women

Chest for offerings

THE TEMPLE HAD VAST WEALTH: IT CAME FROM THE OFFERINGS WHICH FLOWED IN FROM ALL OVER THE ROMAN EMPIRE AND THE TAXES PROVIDED FOR BY THE LAW. BUT THE COST OF BUILDING AND MAINTENANCE AND THE EXPENSE OF THE SERVICES WERE VAST. THE TEMPLE DOMINATED THE LIFE OF THE CITY. IN JERUSALEM ALMOST EIGHT OUT OF TEN OF THE INHABITANTS LIVED OFF THE TEMPLE: PRIESTS, LEVITES, CRAFTSMEN, TRADERS, WORKERS . . .

59

HOW DO YOU SEE THE RELIGIOUS LIFE?

FOR ME IT'S LOOKING UP AT THE SKY AND EXPECTING GOD TO PERFORM A MIRACLE

FOR ME, IT'S LOOKING AT THE WORLD AND EXPECTING GOD TO DO SOMETHING

BEN! WHILE WE'RE WAITING WE CAN LOOK AT EACH OTHER!

RELIGIOUS LIFE

WHO RAN THE TEMPLE?

IN THE TIME OF THE KINGS, THE **HIGH PRIEST** WAS CHIEF OF THE PRIESTS. LATER, HE BECAME THE RELIGIOUS AND CIVIL LEADER OF THE WHOLE PEOPLE. HE HAD A SPECIAL FUNCTION IN THE CULT AND LED THE MOST IMPORTANT CEREMONIES. HE ALONE HAD THE RIGHT TO ENTER THE 'HOLY OF HOLIES' IN THE TEMPLE ONCE A YEAR. HIS DRESS WAS SPECIAL AND DIFFERED FROM THAT OF THE OTHER PRIESTS.

High priest

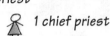

1 commander of the Temple   1 chief priest

7 Temple watchmen

3 treasurers

7,200 priests divided into 24 groups

9,600 Levites divided into 24 groups

THE **PRIESTS** WERE PRESENT AT SACRIFICES, BURNED INCENSE, BLESSED THE PEOPLE, BLEW THE SHOPHAR TO ANNOUNCE THE FESTIVALS AND THE BEGINNING OF THE SABBATH, TENDED THE LAMP IN THE TEMPLE WHICH ALWAYS HAD TO BE ALIGHT, SAW TO THE PURIFICATION OF THE PEOPLE, CHECKED HEALINGS, AND KEPT THE HOLY BOOKS. IN EARLIEST TIMES, THE PRIESTS ENSURED THE ORAL TRANSMISSION OF TEACHING FROM ONE GENERATION TO ANOTHER.

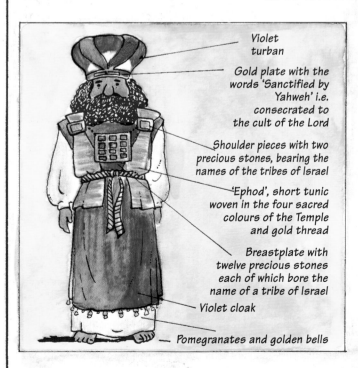

Violet turban

Gold plate with the words 'Sanctified by Yahweh' i.e. consecrated to the cult of the Lord

Shoulder pieces with two precious stones, bearing the names of the tribes of Israel

'Ephod', short tunic woven in the four sacred colours of the Temple and gold thread

Breastplate with twelve precious stones each of which bore the name of a tribe of Israel

Violet cloak

Pomegranates and golden bells

Turban of fine linen

Tunic of costly fine linen

Belt in the four colours of the Temple: violet, purple, scarlet and white

Under the tunic were trousers, again linen, covering the knees

Bare feet

THE LEVITES

THE JERUSALEM TEMPLE ATTRACTED GREAT CROWDS. ITS TREASURE WAS FABULOUS. THE LEVITES HAD TO MOUNT GUARD AT THE TEMPLE GATES, TO KEEP ACCOUNT OF THE OFFERINGS, TO ENGAGE IN BUILDING WORK AND TEMPLE MAINTENANCE, TO BLOW THE TRUMPET AND SING DURING WORSHIP. THE SENIOR CLERGY WERE RICH, BUT ORDINARY PRIESTS AND LEVITES WERE POOR AND BADLY PAID.

IN EARLIEST TIMES, ANY MAN IN ISRAEL COULD BE A PRIEST IN A SANCTUARY. THEN THE KING CHOSE THE PRIESTS. LATER THIS FUNCTION BECAME HEREDITARY. IT WAS RESERVED FOR THE TRIBE OF LEVI. NOT ALL LEVITES WERE PRIESTS, BUT THEY WERE ALL INVOLVED IN RELIGIOUS LIFE, WITH LESS IMPORTANT TASKS. AT THE TIME OF THE ROMAN CONQUEST, THE PRIESTS ADAPTED TO THE NEW SITUATION IN ORDER TO BE ABLE TO MAINTAIN TEMPLE WORSHIP. AT THE END OF THE WAR AGAINST THE ROMANS IN 70, THE TEMPLE WAS DESTROYED AND THE JEWISH PRIESTS DISAPPEARED FOR EVER.

THE DOCTORS OF THE LAW
(OR SCRIBES)

IN EARLIEST TIMES THE PRIESTS WERE RESPONSIBLE FOR TEACHING THE TORAH. LATER, THIS TEACHING WAS DONE IN THE SYNAGOGUES. THE DOCTORS OF THE LAW WERE SCHOLARS RESPONSIBLE FOR INTERPRETING AND TRANSMITTING IT. THEY TAUGHT THE LAW OF MOSES (WRITTEN) AND THE TRADITIONS OF THE ELDERS (ORAL). IT WAS ALSO THEIR RESPONSIBILITY TO COPY THE TORAH.

BEFORE BECOMING TEACHERS (RABBIS) THEY STUDIED FOR MANY YEARS UNDER THE SUPERVISION OF THE GREAT MASTERS. THE DOCTORS OF THE LAW WERE USUALLY POOR BECAUSE THEY OFFERED THEIR KNOWLEDGE FREE. THEY HAD TO PRACTISE A TRADE TO EARN THEIR LIVING. SOMETIMES THEY RECEIVED GIFTS FROM THEIR PUPILS AND HELP FROM THE TEMPLE.

THE SANHEDRIN

THE WORD SANHEDRIN MEANS ASSEMBLY, COUNCIL. IT WAS THE RELIGIOUS, ADMINISTRATIVE AND LEGAL GUIDE FOR THE JEWISH PEOPLE. IT MET IN JERUSALEM.

THE SANHEDRIN WAS PRESIDED OVER BY THE **HIGH PRIEST** AND MADE UP OF SEVENTY-ONE MEMBERS, COMPRISING REPRESENTATIVES OF THE NOBILITY (**ELDERS**), **CHIEF PRIESTS** EITHER SERVING OR RETIRED, AND **DOCTORS OF THE LAW**. ITS JURISDICTION EXTENDED TO ALL JEWS LIVING IN PALESTINE OR ELSEWHERE. THE SANHEDRIN WAS THE SUPREME TRIBUNAL WHICH JUDGED CRIMES AGAINST THE LAW. AS WELL AS THE GREAT SANHEDRIN THERE WERE LITTLE SANHEDRINS, **LOCAL COURTS** RESPONSIBLE FOR SETTLING CURRENT CASES.

THE PROPHETS

THE PROPHETS WERE NOT SOOTHSAYERS BUT BELIEVERS WHO FELT RESPONSIBLE FOR A SPECIAL MISSION ENTRUSTED TO THEM BY THE LORD. THEIR PREACHING WAS NOT ALWAYS THE SAME, SINCE IT WAS ADAPTED TO DIFFERENT SITUATIONS.
THE PROPHETS WANTED THE KINGS, THE POWERFUL AND THE PEOPLE TO REMAIN FAITHFUL TO GOD AND HIS LAW.
THIS MISSION MADE LIFE DIFFICULT AND OFTEN RISKY.

THE BATTLES OF THE PROPHETS

AGAINST IDOLATRY

ISRAEL'S FAITH IN THE ONE GOD WAS NOT ALWAYS FIRM. OVER ITS HISTORY THE PEOPLE MADE CONTACT WITH OTHER POPULATIONS. THUS THEY DISCOVERED OTHER CULTS AND OTHER GODS AND WERE ATTRACTED BY IDOLATRY EITHER THROUGH CONFORMISM OR BY POLITICAL CALCULATION.

Every place or natural phenomenon had its Baal (lord). The **Baal** of the sky ruled over all.

pendant with the image of **Astarte** (or **Asherah**), goddess of fertility

amulet representing **Bes**, an Egyptian, Phoenician and Canaanite deity who protects from evil

THE PROPHET ELIJAH AND THE CULT OF BAAL

AFTER I KINGS 18

During the third year of a terrible drought, King Ahab went to meet Elijah. As soon as he saw him, he cried: 'Is it you, the scourge of Israel?' Elijah replied: 'I am not the scourge of Israel, but you and your family are because you have abandoned the commandments of the Lord and worshipped the idols of Baal!'

AGAINST THE TYRANNY OF THE KINGS

KING DAVID SEDUCED THE WIFE OF HIS FAITHFUL OFFICER URIAH AND MADE SURE THAT URIAH WAS KILLED IN BATTLE.

TO GET HOLD OF A VINEYARD, KING AHAB HAD ITS OWNER EXECUTED AFTER A TRIAL BASED ON FALSE WITNESSES.

FROM II SAMUEL 12

Nathan says to David:
'Hear what the Lord God of Israel says to you: I consecrated you king over Israel . . . Why then did you scorn the Lord, doing what is evil in his sight? You have struck Uriah the Hittite with the sword; you have taken his wife as your own. From now on the sword will not cease to strike your house, to punish you because you have scorned me.'

FROM I KINGS 21

On the orders of the Lord, Elijah the Tishbite went to the king of Israel. When Ahab saw Elijah he said to him, 'Have you found me, O my enemy?' Elijah replied, 'Yes, I have found you. Since you have dishonored yourself doing what is evil in the eyes of the Lord, I will bring misfortune upon you. I will sweep away your descendants and exterminate all the males of your house.'

AGAINST INJUSTICE

AFTER AMOS 2

Thus says Yahweh: 'The inhabitants of Israel have committed so many crimes. I shall punish them. They have sold honest men as slaves since they could not pay their debts . . . They trample the poor in the dust and make the life of the weak very harsh.'

AGAINST FALSE CERTAINTIES

AFTER JEREMIAH 7

Jeremiah stops before the entrance to the Temple and addresses the following words to those going in: 'Hear what the Lord of the universe, the God of Israel, says to you. "Change your ways and I will let you live in this place. But you steal, you offer sacrifices to Baal and worship strange gods. And now you come to this Temple which is consecrated to me, and you say, we are safe, and then you do the same things all over again. Do you take this Temple to be a robber's den?"'

THE SYNAGOGUE

THE JEWS COULD NOT GO TO THE TEMPLE REGULARLY. AFTER THE EXILE, EVEN IF THE TEMPLE RETAINED ITS IMPORTANCE, THE JEWS INSIDE AND OUTSIDE PALESTINE GRADUALLY DEVELOPED THE CUSTOM IN VILLAGES AND TOWNS - INCLUDING JERUSALEM - OF MEETING IN PLACES CALLED 'SYNAGOGUES' OR 'HOUSES OF PRAYER'. OVER THE CENTURIES SYNAGOGUES UNDERWENT AN ENORMOUS EXPANSION. ONLY TEN MEN WERE NEEDED TO FOUND A SYNAGOGUE.

A village with its synagogue on Lake Tiberias at the time of the Roman empire

THE SYNAGOGUE WAS OPEN ALL DAY AND SERVED AS A SCHOOL FOR THE YOUNG. IT WAS ALSO THE CENTER OF THE VILLAGE. PEOPLE MET THERE TO DISCUSS PUBLIC AND PRIVATE MATTERS, THE PROBLEMS OF VILLAGE LIFE. ON MARKET DAYS, A SMALL TRIBUNAL - THE SANHEDRIN - MET TO SETTLE MINOR CASES.

A CENTER OF SOCIAL LIFE

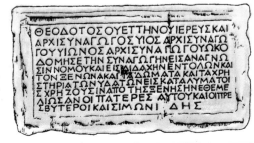

GREEK INSCRIPTION IN A JERUSALEM SYNAGOGUE (FIRST CENTURY AD): 'THEODOTUS, SON OF ONE OF THE LEADERS OF THE COMMUNITY, BUILT THE SYNAGOGUE TO PROMOTE THE READING OF THE LAW OF THE LORD . . . AND BUILT THE INN FOR TRAVELLERS AND ROOMS TO WELCOME STRANGERS IN NEED . . .'

THE BUILDING

The cupboard with the scrolls of the law is orientated on Jerusalem

Place reserved for women and children

There was often a school in the courtyard of a synagogue

The seven-branched lampstand is the same as that in the Temple

Dais for reading the Torah

Jars for ritual ablutions

THE ORGANIZATION

THE **LOCAL COMMUNITY** GOVERNED THE SYNAGOGUE. A **COUNCIL OF ELDERS** WAS CHOSEN FROM AMONG ITS MEMBERS, WHICH INCLUDED THE **RULER OF THE SYNAGOGUE**. THERE WAS ALWAYS A **CARETAKER**. THE RULER OF THE SYNAGOGUE WAS RESPONSIBLE FOR THE REGULAR WORSHIP. THERE WERE NEITHER PRIESTS NOR SACRIFICES IN THE SYNAGOGUES. THEY WERE TO BE FOUND ONLY IN THE TEMPLE.

THE WORSHIP

IT BEGAN WITH THE PRAYER '**SHEMA ISRAEL**' (HEAR, O ISRAEL) AND **INVOCATIONS** AND **BLESSINGS** PRONOUNCED BY THE RULER OF THE SYNAGOGUE. THE COMMUNITY RESPONDED '**AMEN**', WHICH MEANS 'THAT IS CERTAIN'. THEN THE CARETAKER BROUGHT THE SCROLL OF THE **TORAH** OUT OF THE CUPBOARD AND GAVE IT TO THE PERSON WHO WAS TO READ. HE WAS FORBIDDEN TO RECITE THE LAW BY HEART, AS THE TEXT COULD NOT BE CHANGED. THE READING WAS DONE IN HEBREW, BUT EACH TIME IT WAS TRANSLATED INTO THE LOCAL LANGUAGE BY AN INTERPRETER SO THAT EVERYONE COULD UNDER-STAND. THEN CAME THE **READING OF THE PROPHETS** AND THE **TEACHING**. EVERY MEMBER OF THE COMMUNITY (EVEN THE NEWEST ARRIVAL) HAD THE RIGHT TO SPEAK IN ORDER TO GIVE HIS COMMENTARY (MARK 1. 2; LUKE 4. 15ff.; ACTS 13. 14–15). WORSHIP ENDED WITH **PRAYER** AND A **BLESSING**.

THE DIASPORA

JEWS WHO FOR SOME REASON HAD SETTLED ABROAD FORMED THE DIASPORA (THE WORD IS GREEK AND MEANS 'DISPERSION'). THE FIRST SMALL GROUPS FORMED IN EGYPT AND BABYLON AT THE TIME OF THE EXILE AND OTHER GROUPS WERE TO BE FOUND LATER IN SYRIA, ASIA AND ROME.
THE SYNAGOGUE WAS VERY IMPORTANT FOR PEOPLE LIVING A LONG WAY FROM THEIR HOMELAND AND THE TEMPLE. IT FORMED A BIT OF THE LAND OF ISRAEL. THAT IS WHY JEWISH HOUSES WERE BUILT NEAR THE SYNAGOGUE AND WHEN A JEW ARRIVED IN A STRANGE CITY HE WENT TO THE SYNAGOGUE, WHERE HE WAS SURE TO FIND A WELCOME AND HELP IF NECESSARY (ACTS 13. 14–15; 17. 1–3; 18. 1–4).

BEFORE GOD, IS IT BETTER TO BE ONE OF THE CROWD OR AN INDIVIDUAL?

IN A CROWD EVERYONE IS SO 'EQUAL' THAT IT'S IMPOSSIBLE TO DISTINGUISH ONE FROM THE OTHER

AN INDIVIDUAL IS SO UNPREDICTABLE AND SELFISH ...

WHAT IF GOD PREFERS SMALL MEDITATION GROUPS?

JEWISH GROUPS

THE SADDUCEES

THE JERUSALEM PRIESTS AND LEVITES AND THE RICH AND POWERFUL BELONGED TO THIS TREND. THE SADDUCEES BASED THEMSELVES FIRMLY ON SCRIPTURE. FOR THEM, THE **FIRST FIVE BOOKS** OF THE BIBLE HAD AN ABSOLUTE VALUE AND HAD TO BE TAKEN LITERALLY. SO THEY DID NOT ACCEPT EITHER THE IDEA OF **RESURRECTION**, WHICH DOES NOT APPEAR IN THE PENTATEUCH, OR THE **COMMENTARIES** BY THE DOCTORS OF THE LAW. FOR THE SADDUCEES, **THE TEMPLE AND ITS SACRIFICES** WERE THE CENTER OF FAITH. IN ORDER NOT TO LOSE IT, THEY **SUBMITTED** TO **ROMAN** POLITICAL POLICY. HOWEVER, THE PEOPLE DID NOT LIKE THE POLITICAL AND RELIGIOUS LEADERS BEING TOO CONCILIATORY TO THE INVADERS.

THE PHARISEES

FOR THE PHARISEES, **RESPECT FOR THE LAW** WAS THE CENTER OF LIFE. THEY WERE VERY METICULOUS IN FOLLOWING THE PRECEPTS OF THE LAW AND THE ORAL TRADITION. THEY AVOIDED CONTACT WITH ALL THOSE WHO COULD NOT OR DID NOT WANT TO LIVE LIKE THEM. FOR THIS REASON THEY WERE **HOSTILE TO THE ROMANS**. MOST PHARISEES LOOKED FOR LIBERATION BY THE DIRECT INTERVENTION OF GOD, SO THEY DID NOT ACTIVELY OPPOSE ROMAN DOMINATION.

EVERY PHARISEE HOPED THAT IF THE PEOPLE PREPARED THEMSELVES IN PURITY AND HOLINESS, THE **MESSIAH** - THE MESSENGER OF THE LORD - WOULD APPEAR, TO PURGE JERUSALEM OF THE PAGANS AND GOVERN IN **JUSTICE**. IN THE TIME OF JESUS, THE PHARISEES RECEIVED TREMENDOUS SUPPORT FROM THE PEOPLE WHO, FOR RELIGIOUS, POLITICAL AND ECONOMIC REASONS, FOUND IT VERY DIFFICULT TO SUPPORT THE ROMAN DOMINATION

THE ZEALOTS

THE ZEALOTS WERE UNWILLING TO WAIT FOR GOD'S INTERVENTION TO BRING FREEDOM. THEY WANTED TO PROVOKE A **REBELLION AGAINST THE ROMAN ARMY**. THE STRUGGLE BEGAN WITH GUERRILLA WARFARE AND LATER BECAME OPEN REVOLT. IT ENDED WITH WAR AND THE DESTRUCTION OF JERUSALEM BY THE ROMANS.

THE ESSENES

THE ESSENES LIVED APART FROM THE WORLD, IN THE DESERT, NEAR THE DEAD SEA. THEY WOULD NOT COMPROMISE IN ANY WAY WITH THE PAGAN WORLD AND OBSERVED ALL THE LAWS OF MOSES. THEY REJECTED THE TEMPLE SACRIFICES AND AWAITED THE END OF THE WORLD AND GOD'S JUDGMENT. MANUSCRIPTS OF AN ESSENE COMMUNITY HAVE BEEN FOUND IN THE CAVES OF QUMRAN. THESE WRITINGS CONTAIN PRAYERS, HYMNS AND COMMENTARIES ON THE OLD TESTAMENT AND THE COMMUNITY'S RULE OF LIFE. TO BECOME A MEMBER ONE HAD TO GIVE UP EVERYTHING: HOME, FAMILY, WORK. THE LIFE OF THE ESSENES WAS REGULATED BY AN UNCHANGEABLE CALENDAR AND CONTROLLED BY THE MOST IMPORTANT PERSON IN THE COMMUNITY, CALLED 'THE TEACHER OF RIGHTEOUSNESS.'

THE DISCIPLES OF JOHN THE BAPTIST

WERE USUALLY ORDINARY PEOPLE. THEY WERE OFTEN DISSATISFIED WITH RELIGION AS PRACTICED IN THE TEMPLE. NEAR THE JORDAN RIVER, JOHN THE BAPTIST PREACHED AN IMMINENT JUDGMENT AND THAT UNREPENTANT PEOPLE WOULD BE LIABLE TO PUNISHMENT. REPENTANCE AND A CHANGE OF LIFE WERE EXPRESSED BY BAPTISM, I.E., IMMERSION IN WATER, SIGNIFYING PURIFICATION OF THE HEART.

THE SAMARITANS

LIVED IN THE CENTRAL AREA OF PALESTINE AND FORMED A COMMUNITY DISTINCT FROM ISRAEL. THEY HAD THEIR TEMPLE ON MOUNT GERIZIM, WITH THEIR OWN RITES AND PRIESTS.
THEY ACCEPTED ONLY THE PENTATEUCH AS A HOLY BOOK AND AWAITED THE COMING OF THE MESSIAH, WHOM THEY THOUGHT TO BE LIKE MOSES.
THE SAMARITANS DID NOT BELONG TO THE JEWISH COMMUNITIES.
SAMARITANS AND JEWS SCORNED AND DETESTED EACH OTHER.

THE PEOPLE

FROM EARLIEST TIMES, THE PEOPLE OF ISRAEL LOOKED FOR A PEACEFUL FUTURE FOR ALL.
THIS HOPE SOMETIMES TOOK ON THE ASPECT OF A JUST RULER FROM THE HOUSE OF DAVID. SOMETIMES IT WAS HOPED THAT GOD HIMSELF WOULD RULE OVER EVERYTHING.

ALTERNATIVELY, THE PEOPLE EXPECTED SOMEONE SENT BY THE LORD. IN THE TIME OF JESUS, THIS EXPECTATION WAS SHARED BY MUCH OF THE WORLD. BUT PEOPLE THOUGHT ABOVE ALL OF A LIBERATOR WHO WOULD DRIVE OUT THE ROMANS. FALSE EXPECTATIONS AND HOPES WERE FAR MORE LIVELY AMONG THE POOR AND OPPRESSED THAN AMONG THE RULING CLASSES OF JERUSALEM.

DO YOU KNOW, I'VE DISCOVERED THAT THE BIBLE IS MADE UP OF VARIOUS WRITINGS BY VARIOUS AUTHORS FROM DIFFERENT TIMES

ALL THE ORIGINALS HAVE BEEN LOST AND WHAT HAVE COME DOWN TO US ARE ONLY COPIES OF COPIES

DOES THAT SURPRISE YOU?
NOT AT ALL

AS YOU KNOW, I'VE DISCOVERED THAT I'M A NINJA TURTLE!

WHAT IS THE BIBLE? 1

YOUR BIBLE IS WRITTEN IN ENGLISH AND HAS BEEN PRINTED RECENTLY. BUT DO YOU KNOW THAT IT IS A VERY

ANCIENT

BOOK WITH A

LONG

HISTORY AND LOTS OF

ADVENTURES

THE WORD BIBLE COMES FROM THE GREEK βιβλία WHICH MEANS 'BOOKS'

THE BIBLE IS IN FACT A COLLECTION OF BOOKS WRITTEN AT **DIFFERENT** TIMES ON **DIFFERENT** SUBJECTS. THE EARLIEST WERE WRITTEN MORE THAN **2,500** YEARS AGO, THE LATEST AROUND **1,900** YEARS AGO.

THE AUTHORS

THERE ARE VERY MANY OF THEM, WRITING BY HAND, OFTEN UNKNOWN. THEY RARELY GIVE INFORMATION ABOUT THEMSELVES.

wrote on PAPYRUS

PAPYRUS IS A PLANT WHICH GROWS IN WATER. ITS STALKS ARE CUT INTO FINE STRIPS.

THE STRIPS ARE LAID OUT IN TWO PERPENDICULAR LAYERS.

THE TWO LAYERS ARE COVERED WITH FABRIC AND HAMMERED . . .

or on PARCHMENT

A VERY TOUGH MATERIAL MADE FROM THE SKIN OF SHEEP AND GOATS. AFTER BEING WORKED ON AND TREATED IT HAS BECOME SUPPLE AND CAN BE WRITTEN ON.

. . . AND THEN SMOOTHED OUT. BY JOINING SEVERAL LEAVES TOGETHER IT IS POSSIBLE TO MAKE PAPYRUS SCROLLS.

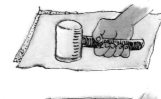

A LONG JOURNEY

ALL THE MANUSCRIPTS HAVE BEEN LOST!

THEN HOW DID THE BIBLE COME DOWN TO US?

some discoveries

1902 A VERY ANCIENT COPY OF THE OLD TESTAMENT WAS FOUND IN EGYPT, WELL PRESERVED IN THE DRY SAND.

1920 A VERY SMALL PAPYRUS WAS FOUND IN EGYPT, WRITTEN IN GREEK, CONTAINING PART OF THE GOSPEL OF JOHN CH. 18. SO FAR, IT IS THE EARLIEST FRAGMENT OF THE NEW TESTAMENT TO HAVE BEEN DISCOVERED.

1947 IN THE SPRING, SEVERAL BEDOUINS WERE GRAZING THEIR SHEEP NEAR THE DEAD SEA. A YOUNG MAN, MUHAMMAD, 'THE WOLF', WAS LOOKING FOR A LOST GOAT. HE THREW STONES INTO A DARK CAVE. NO BLEATING, BUT THE SOUND OF A BROKEN POT. THE YOUNG MAN RAN OFF IN FRIGHT.
HE RETURNED TO THE CAVE WITH A FRIEND AND THERE FOUND EIGHT JARS WITH COVERINGS. INSIDE HE FOUND LONG OBJECTS: THESE WERE ANCIENT MANUSCRIPTS CONTAINING BIBLICAL AND OTHER TEXTS. THEY HAD PROBABLY BEEN HIDDEN TO KEEP THEM SAFE FROM THE ROMANS DURING THE JEWISH WAR (AD 66-70).

FORTUNATELY, MANY COPIES OF THE ORIGINALS HAD BEEN MADE TO CIRCULATE THEM TO AS MANY PEOPLE AS POSSIBLE.

OVER THE CENTURIES, COPYISTS KEPT COPYING THE TEXT . . .

IN THE TABLE OF CONTENTS OF EVERY BIBLE WE FIND A DIVISION BETWEEN OLD TESTAMENT (**JEWISH BIBLE**) AND NEW TESTAMENT.
MOST OF THE BOOKS OF THE OLD TESTAMENT WERE **WRITTEN IN HEBREW** BY **JEWISH AUTHORS**.
THE BOOKS OF THE NEW TESTAMENT WERE **WRITTEN IN GREEK** BY **CHRISTIAN AUTHORS**.
JESUS READ THE OLD TESTAMENT AND KNEW IT WELL. IT WAS WRITTEN BY HAND ON SEVERAL PARCHMENT SCROLLS.

IN THE MIDDLE AGES, THE MONKS COPIED THE MANUSCRIPTS. THEY OFTEN DECORATED THEM WITH VERY COLORFUL AND ILLUSTRATED LETTERS.

WHAT IS THE BIBLE? 2

THE JOURNEY CONTINUES . . .

IN 1456, GUTENBERG, A GERMAN PRINTER, INVENTED MOVABLE CHARACTERS FOR PRINTING. THE FIRST IMPORTANT WORK TO BE PRINTED WAS THE **BIBLE**

THE FIRST PRINTED BIBLE WAS WRITTEN IN LATIN, THE LANGUAGE OF THE CHURCH, EDUCATED PEOPLE AND THE RICH . . .

WHAT ABOUT THE REST?

THE FIRST COMPLETE ENGLISH TRANSLATION OF THE BIBLE, BY MILES COVERDALE, WAS PRINTED IN 1535. HOWEVER, THE FIRST COMPLETE ITALIAN TRANSLATION HAD ALREADY BEEN PRINTED IN VENICE IN 1471.

IN 1521 LUTHER TRANSLATED THE BIBLE INTO GERMAN SO THAT READING IT WAS NOT THE PRIVILEGE OF A SMALL MINORITY.

TODAY, GROUPS TO STUDY THE BIBLE MEET IN LARGE NUMBERS IN TOWN AND COUNTRY.

70 TODAY, THE BIBLE HAS BEEN TRANSLATED INTO MORE THAN A THOUSAND LANGUAGES AND DIALECTS ALL OVER THE WORLD.

TO KNOW MORE

THE LABELS ON THE SIDES OF THE SHELVES SHOW THAT THE BIBLE DEALS WITH A GREAT MANY SUBJECTS.

YOU WILL SEE MANY NAMES WRITTEN ON THE BOOKS, BUT THE AUTHORS ARE OFTEN UNKNOWN.

IN FACT, THEY OFTEN BORROWED THE NAMES OF MEN FAMOUS FOR THEIR FAITH (LIKE THE PROPHETS OR THE APOSTLES), NOT TO BENEFIT THEMSELVES BUT TO HONOR THEM.

HOWEVER, SOME AUTHORS ARE KNOWN AND WE HAVE VARIOUS INFORMATION ABOUT THEM.

THE PROPHET JEREMIAH IS DICTATING TO HIS SECRETARY.

HERE ARE FOUR BOOKS AND FOUR STORIES THAT YOU KNOW WELL. OFTEN THE BIBLE WAS FIRST HANDED DOWN ORALLY AND ONLY LATER PUT INTO WRITING.

THE APOSTLE PAUL IS WRITING TO HIS FRIENDS IN THE FIRST CHRISTIAN COMMUNITIES.

PLACES, FACTS AND IDEAS

73

... IN THE TIME OF ABRAHAM

ARE YOU AND I PART OF THE FLORA AND FAUNA?

CERTAINLY, ALL THE PLANTS ARE PART OF THE FLORA ...

AND ALL THE ANIMALS ARE PART OF THE FAUNA

WHAT ARE YOU DOING? I'M A PLANT!

CLIMATE, FLORA, FAUNA

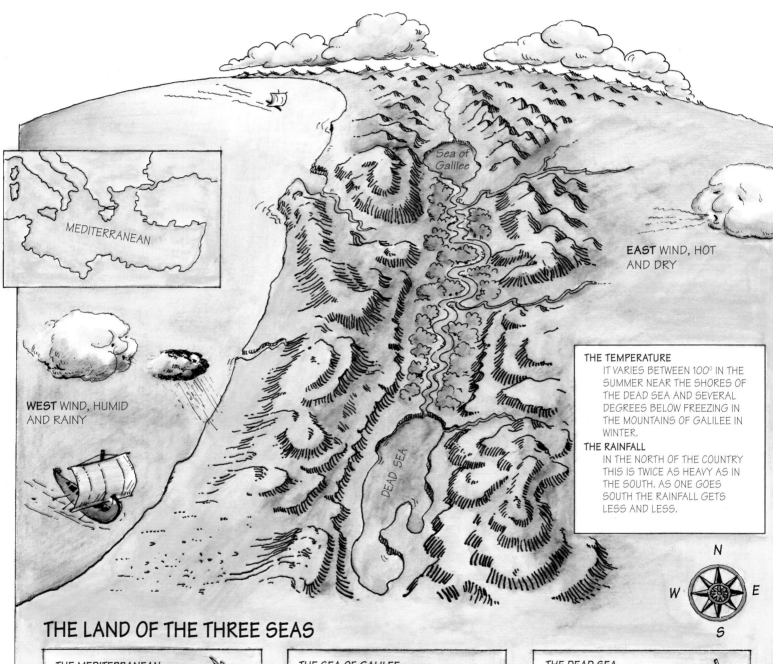

MEDITERRANEAN

Sea of Galilee

EAST WIND, HOT AND DRY

WEST WIND, HUMID AND RAINY

DEAD SEA

THE TEMPERATURE
IT VARIES BETWEEN 100° IN THE SUMMER NEAR THE SHORES OF THE DEAD SEA AND SEVERAL DEGREES BELOW FREEZING IN THE MOUNTAINS OF GALILEE IN WINTER.

THE RAINFALL
IN THE NORTH OF THE COUNTRY THIS IS TWICE AS HEAVY AS IN THE SOUTH. AS ONE GOES SOUTH THE RAINFALL GETS LESS AND LESS.

N W E S

THE LAND OF THE THREE SEAS

THE MEDITERRANEAN

THE JEWS WERE NOT GREAT SAILORS LIKE THE PHOENICIANS. FOR THE JEWS THE SEA SYMBOLIZED DANGER. FISHING IN THE SEA WAS ALMOST NON-EXISTENT.

THE SEA OF GALILEE

THE LAKE WAS RICH IN FISH WITH GREEN SHORES WHERE THERE WERE FISHING TOWNS AND VILLAGES.

THE DEAD SEA

SITUATED IN A DEEP DEPRESSION WITH WATER RICH IN MINERAL SALTS WHICH PREVENT ANY FORM OF LIFE.

A MEDITERRANEAN COUNTRY

IN PALESTINE, THE SUMMER IS LONG, VERY HOT AND DRY.

THE WINTER IS SHORT, WARM AND RAINY. THE RAIN IS IRREGULAR.

IN THE TIME OF JESUS, THE COUNTRY LIVED BY AGRICULTURE ON LAND SNATCHED FROM THE DESERT, WAITING FOR RAIN.

HILLY LAND WAS PROTECTED BY STONE WALLS IN A STRUGGLE AGAINST EROSION.

THERE WAS A PERPETUAL LACK OF WATER

AND A CONSTANT THREAT OF INVASIONS BY LOCUSTS.

WOLF

BEAR

GAZELLE

LION

THE ONLY RIVER IS ENCLOSED IN SUCH A DEEP DEPRESSION THAT IT IS DIFFICULT TO USE ITS WATER. THIS FLOWS DOWN TO THE DEAD SEA WHERE, BECAUSE OF THE HEAT, IT EVAPORATES. THE VALLEY IS RICH IN DENSE VEGETATION AND VARIOUS WILD ANIMALS LIVE THERE, SOME OF THEM FIERCE.

DOMESTIC ANIMALS

TREES AND FLOWERS

CEDAR OF LEBANON

EDIBLE PLANTS

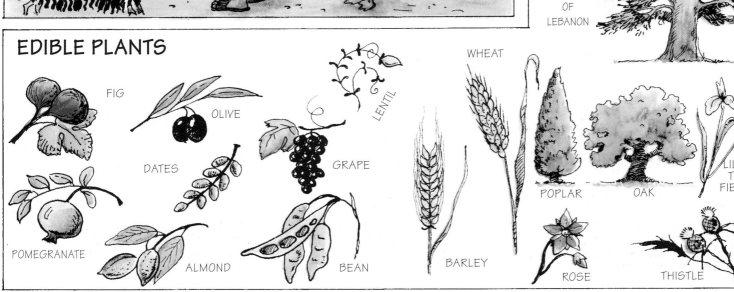

FIG

OLIVE

DATES

LENTIL

WHEAT

GRAPE

POPLAR

OAK

LILY OF THE FIELDS

POMEGRANATE

ALMOND

BEAN

BARLEY

ROSE

THISTLE

FACING A PENDULUM I FEEL A DEEP ANXIETY

AT EVERY MOTION OF THE HAND, TIME SLIPS BY ...

SUNDIALS ARE MUCH BETTER: WHEN THE SKY IS CLOUDY, TIME STOPS!

TIME AND THE CALENDAR

Gathering summer fruits

Gathering olives and grapes

Sowing and ploughing

GREAT HEAT

FIRST RAINS

Vine dressing

Growth

ABUNDANT RAINS

Wheat and barley harvest

LAST RAINS

Flax harvest

TAMMUZ · AB · ELUL · TISHRI · MARHESH-WAN · KISLEV · TEBETH · SHEBAT · ADAR · NISAN (Abib) · IYYAR (Ziv) · SIWAN

July · August · September · October · November · December · January · February · March · April · May · June

ACCORDING TO GENESIS 1. 14, GOD CREATED THE SUN AND THE MOON 'TO DIVIDE THE DAY FROM THE NIGHT,' TO SERVE AS 'SIGNS TO MARK THE FESTIVALS, THE DAYS AND THE YEARS.' THE CALCULATION OF TIME WAS LINKED TO THEM.

THE DAY, WHICH IS THE EASIEST UNIT TO OBSERVE AND WHICH REGULATES PUBLIC AND PRIVATE ACTIVITIES, WAS TAKEN AS A BASIC UNIT FOR CALCULATING TIME. HOWEVER, THERE WERE TWO METHODS, STARTING WITH THE **SUN** AND STARTING WITH THE **MOON**, AND THEY DID NOT COINCIDE. IN A PRIMITIVE SOCIETY THESE DIFFERENCES DID NOT MATTER MUCH, BUT WITH THE DEVELOPMENT OF CIVIL, POLITICAL AND RELIGIOUS ACTIVITIES, IT BECAME IMPORTANT TO FIX DATES, I.E. TO ESTABLISH AN OFFICIAL CALENDAR.

METHODS VARIED DEPENDING ON THE TIME AND THE RELIGION. THIS WAS ESPECIALLY TRUE OF ISRAEL, WHICH WAS ALWAYS IN CONTACT WITH DIFFERENT CIVILIZATIONS. IN ANCIENT TIMES, THE YEAR BEGAN IN THE AUTUMN, THE FIRST DAY OF THE MONTH OF TISHRI, BUT LATER IT BEGAN IN SPRING, WITH THE MONTH OF NISAN.

THE MONTH

FROM THE AGRICULTURAL GEZER CALENDAR (TENTH CENTURY BC) WE KNOW THAT THE JEWS HAD A YEAR OF TWELVE MONTHS. IN THE BIBLE, TO FIX A DATE, REFERENCE WAS MADE TO THE YEAR OF A KING'S REIGN OR, LATER, TO AN IMPORTANT MORE OR LESS CONTEMPORARY EVENT. FOR EXAMPLE, THE PROPHECY OF THE PROPHET AMOS IS DATED AT 'TWO YEARS BEFORE THE EARTHQUAKE' (AMOS 1. 1).

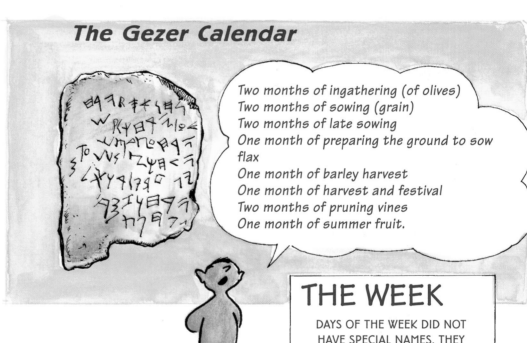

The Gezer Calendar

Two months of ingathering (of olives)
Two months of sowing (grain)
Two months of late sowing
One month of preparing the ground to sow flax
One month of barley harvest
One month of harvest and festival
Two months of pruning vines
One month of summer fruit.

THE DAY

IN THE TIME OF JESUS, EVERY NEW DAY BEGAN THE EVENING BEFORE, AT SUNSET. THE HOURS OF THE DAY (HOURS OF DAYLIGHT) WERE COUNTED FROM SUNRISE TO SUNSET. THE DAY WAS DIVIDED INTO TWELVE PARTS. FOR EXAMPLE, THE THIRD HOUR (MATTHEW 20. 3) WAS ROUGHLY NINE IN THE MORNING. FOR REGULAR USE THE DAY WAS ONLY ROUGHLY DIVIDED, DEPENDING ON NATURAL PHENOMENA: THE MORNING, THE EVENING, SUNSET, WHEN THE NIGHT WIND BLEW, THE HOTTEST HOUR OF THE DAY . . .

THE WEEK

DAYS OF THE WEEK DID NOT HAVE SPECIAL NAMES. THEY WERE ONLY GIVEN NUMBERS, EXCEPT FOR THE SEVENTH, WHICH AS A FESTIVAL WAS NAMED THE SABBATH.

When are you coming back?

When the night breeze blows

. . . BUT NUMEROUS ARCHAEOLOGICAL DISCOVERIES SHOW THAT AS EARLY AS 1000 BC HOUR GLASSES, SUNDIALS AND GNOMONS WERE USED TO TELL THE TIME.

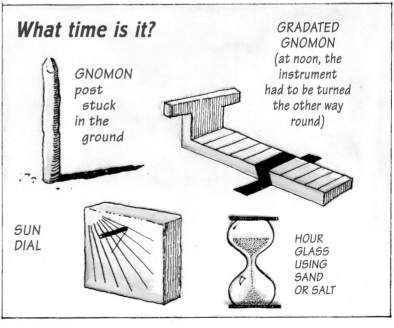

What time is it?

GNOMON post stuck in the ground

GRADATED GNOMON (at noon, the instrument had to be turned the other way round)

SUN DIAL

HOUR GLASS USING SAND OR SALT

IN ISRAEL, THEY DUG OUT BIG CISTERNS TO HOLD WATER

SO THE WOMEN WENT UP AND DOWN STEPS TO GET THE WATER

JUST LIKE ME IN TOWN ...

...I HAVE TO GO **200** MILES TO GET A BREATH OF FRESH AIR

THE DESERT AND WATER

THE MAIN FEATURE OF THE DESERT IS THAT THE LAND DOES NOT RETAIN WATER. IN SUCH HIGH TEMPERATURES HUMAN BEINGS CANNOT SURVIVE EVEN A DAY WITHOUT WATER. HOWEVER, SOME SHRUBS AND ANIMALS CAN FIND MEANS OF SURVIVAL.

The pyramid rat or the kangaroo rat only goes out at night, when it is cooler. So as not to waste the water in its body, it passes very little urine.

RAT'S BURROW

Blocked opening to keep the den moist

Store of grain

FOR THE ISRAELITES THE DESERT WAS NOT ONLY AN ARID AND ROCKY PLACE, BUT ALSO A PLACE FULL OF MEMORIES, ABOVE ALL OF THE EXODUS FROM EGYPT AND THE ENCOUNTER WITH GOD (EXODUS 5. 1). CERTAINLY THE DESERT WAS A PLACE WHERE FEAR, HUNGER AND THIRST REIGNED, BUT IT WAS ALSO THE PLACE WHERE THE LORD GUIDED AND PROTECTED (DEUTERONOMY 8.15).

THAT IS WHY OVER THE CENTURIES THE DESERT REPRESENTED AN ALTERNATIVE TO THE BUSY LIFE OF THE CITY. THE BIBLE TELLS US THAT JOHN THE BAPTIST WITHDREW INTO THE DESERT TO MEDITATE (MATTHEW 3. 1). JESUS SPENT LONG DAYS IN THE DESERT BEFORE PROCLAIMING THE GOOD NEWS TO HIS CONTEMPORARIES (MATTHEW 4. 1).

THE LAND OF THE JEWS WAS POOR IN WATER. EVERY DROP WAS PRECIOUS. IT WAS SOUGHT, COLLECTED AND TRANSPORTED BY TECHNIQUES WHICH REQUIRED MUCH EFFORT AND HARD WORK.

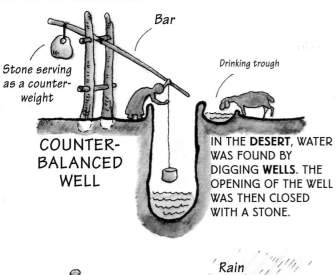

Bar

Stone serving as a counter-weight

Drinking trough

COUNTER-BALANCED WELL

IN THE **DESERT**, WATER WAS FOUND BY DIGGING **WELLS**. THE OPENING OF THE WELL WAS THEN CLOSED WITH A STONE.

Rain

Collecting basin

WHEN THERE WAS NO SPRING, RAINWATER WAS COLLECTED IN CISTERNS.

GETTING WATER WAS THE WORK OF WOMEN AND CHILDREN. SO THE WELL AND DRINKING TROUGH BECAME THE CENTER OF THE VILLAGE. IT WAS A PLACE TO CHAT, TO EXCHANGE NEWS AND TO MAKE THE FIRST CONTACT WITH TRAVELLERS.

IN **CITIES**, TUNNELS AND UNDERGROUND CANALS WERE DUG FOR COLLECTING SPRING WATER.

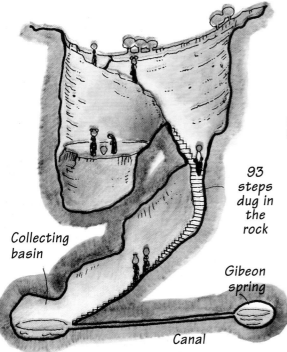

Collecting basin

93 steps dug in the rock

Gibeon spring

Canal

Jerusalem

Pool of Siloam

A tunnel more than 500 yards long which King Hezekiah had dug 2,700 years ago.

Gihon spring

AFTER CONQUERING PALESTINE, THE ROMANS BUILT **AQUEDUCTS** TO SERVE THE GREAT CITIES. THE PICTURE IS OF THE AQUEDUCT BETWEEN MOUNT CARMEL AND CAESAREA.

WATER WAS RARE AND PRECIOUS, BUT TO REFUSE A CUP OF WATER TO SOMEONE WAS UNTHINKABLE. IN FAMILIES, WASHING ONE'S HANDS AT CERTAIN TIMES OF DAY TOOK ON SPECIAL SIGNIFICANCE. PEOPLE FELT READY FOR A NEW START, READY TO PRAY AND PRAISE THE LORD. THE BIBLE TELLS US THAT JOHN THE BAPTIST MADE PEOPLE WHO WANTED TO CHANGE THEIR LIVES AND DO THE WILL OF GOD IMMERSE THEMSELVES IN THE RIVER JORDAN.

81

EGYPT: LAND OF REFUGE AND SLAVERY

TWO COUNTRIES, CLOSE BUT . . .

EGYPT

- A GREAT RIVER: THE NILE
- REGULAR INUNDATIONS
- FERTILE MUD DEPOSITED EVERY YEAR
- PLENTIFUL AND ASSURED HARVESTS

CANAAN

- IRREGULAR WINTER RAINS
- YEARS OF GOOD HARVESTS AND YEARS OF MISERY
- FREQUENT FAMINES

THOSE WHO ARRIVED STARVING DISCOVERED EGYPT WITH ITS WELL CULTIVATED LAND, ITS IRRIGATION CANALS RICH IN FISH, THE GREAT RIVER CRISS-CROSSED BY BOATS, THE GRAND BUILDINGS AND A RIGOROUSLY REGIMENTED PEOPLE UNDER THE ABSOLUTE POWER OF THE PHARAOH, A KING REGARDED AS THE SON OF THE SUN GOD.

ABRAHAM took refuge in Egypt
JACOB took refuge in Egypt
But the future of Israel
was not there. For . . .

A SLAVE PEOPLE
LED BY MOSES
REBELLED.

ENOUGH! ENOUGH!
NO MORE!
ENOUGH! NO MORE!

THE LORD
COMMANDS YOU:
LET MY
PEOPLE GO!

IN THE DESERT, ON THE WAY TO CANAAN, ISRAEL WAS TO
BECOME A FREE PEOPLE . . .

Slavery:
Personal subjection . . .

with no freedom whatsoever
and no right
to possessions . . .

INCREDIBLE!
ONLY PRIMITIVE PEOPLE COULD
DO THAT!

. . . abolished in the
nineteenth century

SLAVERY

AMONG PRIMITIVE PEOPLES

THE LOSERS BECAME
SLAVES AND WORKED
FOR THEIR CONQUERORS

IN EGYPT

THE DEVELOPMENT OF
PUBLIC WORKS IN EGYPT
IN PART DEPENDED ON
THE WORK OF SLAVES.
WHILE THE FIELDS WERE
INUNDATED BY THE NILE,
THE PEASANTS WERE
ALSO CONSCRIPTED
TO FORCED LABOUR.
THEY WERE FED AND
PAID WAGES.

PROPERTY OF
NEFER MAAT

THE SLAVES ARE
PRISONERS OF WAR.
ANYONE WHO BUYS
THEM BECOMES
THEIR OWNER AS
ONE BECOMES THE
OWNER OF A CALF
OR A TABLE . . .

IN ROME

 Slaves

 Free
men

In ancient times

During the empire

ROME COULD NOT GET BY WITHOUT
THE UNPAID WORK
OF SLAVES.

UNDER ROMAN LAW
THE SLAVE WAS
HIS MASTER'S
PROPERTY
AND HIS
MASTER COULD
TREAT HIM
AS HE WISHED.

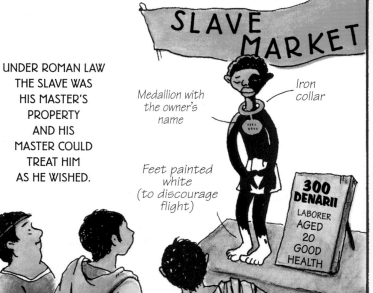

SLAVE
MARKET

*Medallion with
the owner's
name*

*Iron
collar*

*Feet painted
white
(to discourage
flight)*

300
DENARII
LABORER
AGED
20
GOOD
HEALTH

IN ISRAEL

IN **OLD TESTAMENT** TIMES THE SLAVES WERE PRISONERS OF WAR AND FORMED PART OF THE FAMILY WHICH BOUGHT THEM (JUDGES 5. 30; II KINGS 5. 2). THE BIBLE ALSO MENTIONS JEWISH SLAVES (EXODUS 21. 2).

SLAVES WERE NOT OBJECTS BUT MEN AND WOMEN, PROTECTED BY THE **LAW**. THE JEWISH SLAVE SHOULD BE REGARDED AS AN OLDER CHILD AND THE GENTILE SLAVE AS A YOUNGER CHILD.

HEY, NO! today is the Sabbath!

THE SLAVE, WHETHER JEW OR GENTILE, HAS THE RIGHT TO A DAY'S REST (EXODUS 20. 8-10).

ZZZZ... ZZZZ...

MANY IMPORTANT BUILDINGS WERE CONSTRUCTED IN THE TIME OF SOLOMON. MANY ARMS WERE NEEDED. THE KING ESTABLISHED FORCED LABOR IN TEAMS (I SAMUEL 8. 16; I KINGS 5. 27, 28).

...and that makes six years!

THE JEWISH SLAVE WAS FREE AFTER SIX YEARS' WORK. BUT IF HIS SITUATION WAS GOOD HE COULD DECIDE TO STAY PERMANENTLY WITH HIS MASTER (DEUTERONOMY 15. 12-18). EVEN WOMEN WHO HAD BEEN MADE PRISONERS OF WAR WERE PROTECTED BY THE LAW (DEUTERONOMY 21. 10-14).

IN **NEW TESTAMENT** TIMES, SLAVERY WAS NOT VERY WIDESPREAD IN ISRAEL, SINCE FEW PEOPLE WERE RICH. THE SMALL LANDOWNERS, WHO WERE MUCH MORE NUMEROUS, COULD NOT AFFORD THE LUXURY OF SLAVES. ONLY AT COURT WERE THEY USED IN LARGE NUMBERS.

WHEN A JEW BECAME THE SLAVE OF A PAGAN MASTER HE WAS NOT FORGOTTEN BY HIS PEOPLE, WHO DID EVERYTHING POSSIBLE TO REDEEM HIM AS SOON AS THEY COULD.

It's so tiring! If only I had someone to help. But I can't afford a slave. I can barely feed my family.

Today we're going to have a collection to free our brother Ben-Kobba, a slave in Cyrene.

IN THE TIME OF KIING SOLOMON, WHEN PILGRIMS ARRIVED IN JERUSALEM ...

LOOKING UP, THEY SAW ITS RAMPARTS, ITS COLONNADES AND ITS SPLENDID BUILDINGS

WHEN I LOOK UP, I SEE THE RESULTS OF SPECULATIVE BUILDING

JERUSALEM ... IN THE TIME OF THE KINGS

IN THE TIME OF DAVID

WHEN THE ISRAELITES ARRIVED IN THE LAND OF CANAAN, JERUSALEM WAS AN UNIMPORTANT CITY. THEY DID NOT EVEN BOTHER TO OCCUPY IT. DAVID, HOWEVER, FOUND THAT IT MADE AN IDEAL CAPITAL. IT COULD BE EASILY DEFENDED AND IT HAD A SPRING. FURTHERMORE, JERUSALEM WAS SITUATED BETWEEN THE NORTHERN AND SOUTHERN TRIBES.

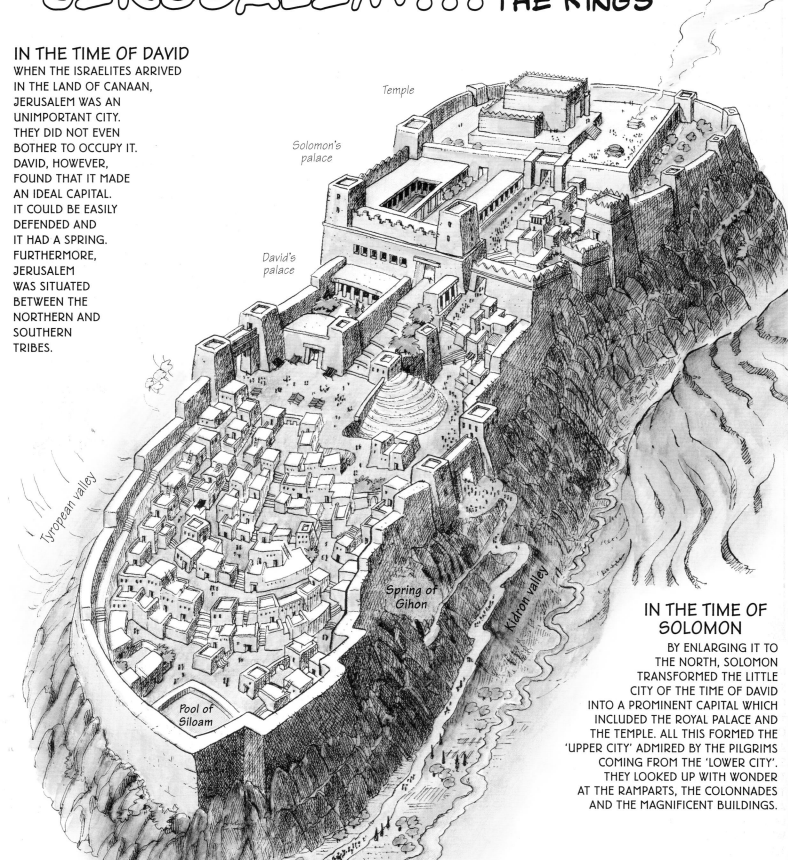

Temple

Solomon's palace

David's palace

Tyropean valley

Spring of Gihon

Kidron valley

Pool of Siloam

IN THE TIME OF SOLOMON

BY ENLARGING IT TO THE NORTH, SOLOMON TRANSFORMED THE LITTLE CITY OF THE TIME OF DAVID INTO A PROMINENT CAPITAL WHICH INCLUDED THE ROYAL PALACE AND THE TEMPLE. ALL THIS FORMED THE 'UPPER CITY' ADMIRED BY THE PILGRIMS COMING FROM THE 'LOWER CITY'. THEY LOOKED UP WITH WONDER AT THE RAMPARTS, THE COLONNADES AND THE MAGNIFICENT BUILDINGS.

THE TEMPLE OF SOLOMON

SOLOMON BEGAN TO BUILD THE TEMPLE ON THE LAND THAT HIS FATHER DAVID HAD BOUGHT YEARS BEFORE FROM ARAUNAH THE JEBUSITE. SOLOMON HAD TRUNKS OF CEDARS OF LEBANON SENT TO HIM BY HIRAM, KING OF TYRE. THESE CAME TO ISRAEL BY SEA AS SO MANY ENORMOUS RAFTS. THEY WERE THEN TRANSPORTED TO JERUSALEM. THE STONE WAS CUT IN THE HILLS OF JUDAEA. THE WOODEN PANELS INSIDE WERE COVERED WITH GOLD AND MUCH COPPER WAS USED TO GIVE THE TEMPLE A SPECTACULAR APPEARANCE. AROUND 100,000 MEN WERE EMPLOYED, ALONG WITH ARCHITECTS AND SPECIALIST WORKERS IN BRONZE. THESE CAME FROM TYRE. THE WORK TOOK SEVEN YEARS.

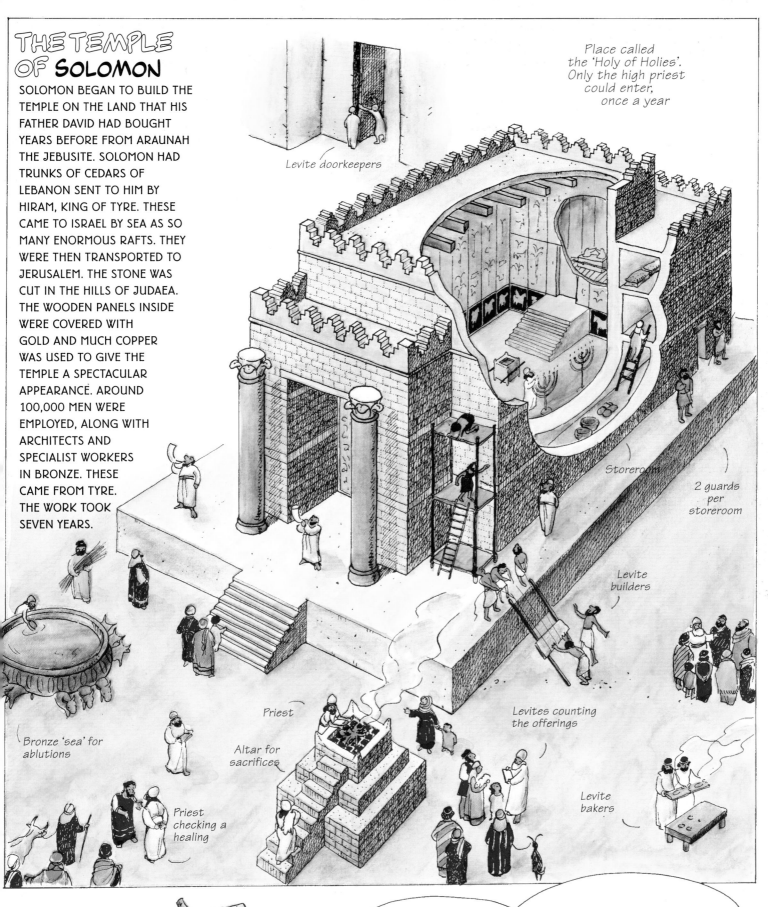

Levite doorkeepers

Place called the 'Holy of Holies'. Only the high priest could enter, once a year

Storeroom

2 guards per storeroom

Levite builders

Levites counting the offerings

Levite bakers

Bronze 'sea' for ablutions

Priest checking a healing

Altar for sacrifices

Priest

IN THE TIME OF SOLOMON, THE FAITH OF ISRAEL BEGAN TO TURN INTO AN OFFICIAL RELIGION AS IN NEIGHBORING STATES. HERE ARE THE WORDS WHICH THE PROPHET JEREMIAH ADDRESSED, RATHER LATER, TO THOSE WHO WERE ENTERING THE TEMPLE:
(JEREMIAH 7. 2B-7A)

ATTENTION!

'Hear the word of the Lord, all you people of Judah who enter these gates to worship the Lord . . . Do not trust in deceptive words, "This is the Temple of the Lord, the Temple of the Lord, the Temple of the Lord." **If** you truly follow the way of goodness and behave well, **if** you practise justice and do not oppress strangers, orphans and widows, **if** in this place you do not condemn the innocent to death or follow strange gods, bringing disaster upon yourselves, I will let you remain in this land . . . .'

AT HIS COURT, KING SOLOMON LIVED WITH ...

700 WIVES AND 300 CONCUBINES ...

... HIS SONS AND HIS DAUGHTERS, HIS SERVANTS AND HIS GUARDS ...

WITH ALL THOSE PEOPLE, WEREN'T THEY CLAUSTROPHOBIC?

AT THE ROYAL COURT

THE KING IS RECEIVING **AMBASSADORS** FROM A FRIENDLY COUNTRY WHO ARE BRINGING VALUABLE GIFTS: GOLD AND SILVER, EMBROIDERED FABRICS, RARE SPICES AND PERFUMES. THE BIBLE MENTIONS EVEN MORE SUMPTUOUS GIFTS: THE KING COULD RECEIVE FLOCKS OF SHEEP AND GOATS AND EVEN VILLAGES AND TOWNS.

THE DELEGATION IS INTRODUCED BY THE **ROYAL HERALD**. HE CONTROLS THE CEREMONY. DURING THE DAYS PRECEDING THE EVENT HE HAS ANNOUNCED THE ARRIVAL OF FOREIGN NOBLES TO THE PEOPLE. THE HERALD REPORTED TO THE SOVEREIGN THE COMMENTS OF HIS SUBJECTS IN THE THRONE ROOM. NOTE ALSO THE KING'S **SECRETARY**, WHO IS ATTENTIVELY WATCHING THE GIFTS, OF WHICH HE WILL MAKE A DETAILED INVENTORY.

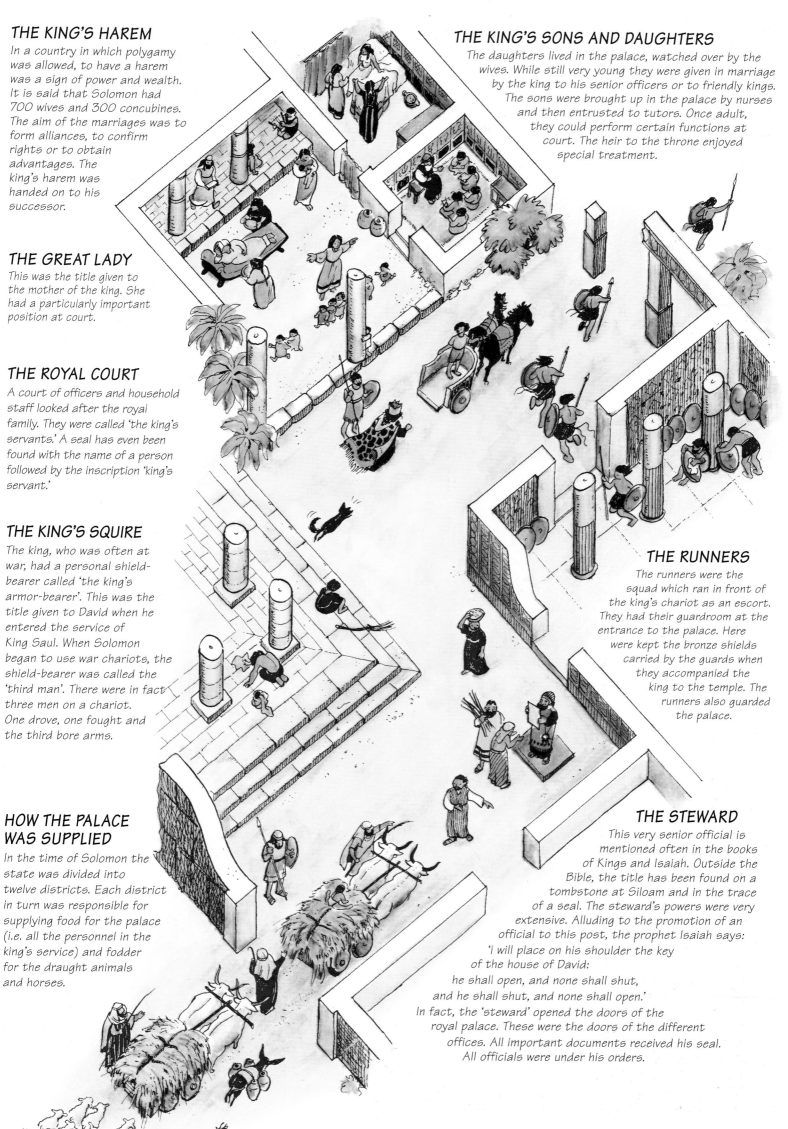

THE KING'S HAREM

In a country in which polygamy was allowed, to have a harem was a sign of power and wealth. It is said that Solomon had 700 wives and 300 concubines. The aim of the marriages was to form alliances, to confirm rights or to obtain advantages. The king's harem was handed on to his successor.

THE GREAT LADY

This was the title given to the mother of the king. She had a particularly important position at court.

THE ROYAL COURT

A court of officers and household staff looked after the royal family. They were called 'the king's servants.' A seal has even been found with the name of a person followed by the inscription 'king's servant.'

THE KING'S SQUIRE

The king, who was often at war, had a personal shield-bearer called 'the king's armor-bearer'. This was the title given to David when he entered the service of King Saul. When Solomon began to use war chariots, the shield-bearer was called the 'third man'. There were in fact three men on a chariot. One drove, one fought and the third bore arms.

HOW THE PALACE WAS SUPPLIED

In the time of Solomon the state was divided into twelve districts. Each district in turn was responsible for supplying food for the palace (i.e. all the personnel in the king's service) and fodder for the draught animals and horses.

THE KING'S SONS AND DAUGHTERS

The daughters lived in the palace, watched over by the wives. While still very young they were given in marriage by the king to his senior officers or to friendly kings. The sons were brought up in the palace by nurses and then entrusted to tutors. Once adult, they could perform certain functions at court. The heir to the throne enjoyed special treatment.

THE RUNNERS

The runners were the squad which ran in front of the king's chariot as an escort. They had their guardroom at the entrance to the palace. Here were kept the bronze shields carried by the guards when they accompanied the king to the temple. The runners also guarded the palace.

THE STEWARD

This very senior official is mentioned often in the books of Kings and Isaiah. Outside the Bible, the title has been found on a tombstone at Siloam and in the trace of a seal. The steward's powers were very extensive. Alluding to the promotion of an official to this post, the prophet Isaiah says:
'I will place on his shoulder the key of the house of David:
he shall open, and none shall shut, and he shall shut, and none shall open.'
In fact, the 'steward' opened the doors of the royal palace. These were the doors of the different offices. All important documents received his seal. All officials were under his orders.

 TODAY I'VE LEARNED THAT IN OLDEN TIMES WHEN PEOPLE WENT TO WAR THEY USED TO PRAY . . .

 . . . THEY OFFERED SACRIFICES AND ASKED FOR GOD'S HELP

 . . .

 TODAY, WE DON'T EVEN HAVE TIME TO THINK. THE WAR IS ALREADY ON THE TV . . .

WAR

The well is ours!

We were there first!

HELP!

IN EARLIEST TIMES, WHEN ISRAEL LED ALMOST A NOMADIC EXISTENCE, THERE WAS NO REAL ARMY. EVERYONE COULD TAKE PART IN A RAID AND HAD TO BE READY TO DEFEND THE TRIBAL PROPERTY.

THE OCCUPATION OF LAND OF THE CANAAN, PARTLY TAKEN FROM THE CANAANITES, WAS NOT THE RESULT OF A MILITARY CONQUEST, BUT THE WORK OF TRIBES OR DETACHED GROUPS WHICH GRADUALLY INFILTRATED THE TERRITORY.

LATER, IN THE TIME OF THE JUDGES, EVERY TIME A PARTICULAR DANGER THREATENED, THE TRIBES UNITED TO CAMPAIGN AGAINST THE DISPOSSESSED CANAANITES WHO WERE REBELLING OR TO DEFEND THEMSELVES AGAINST ATTACKS FROM NEIGHBORING PEOPLES OR NOMADIC RAIDS.

TUUT   TUUT

HEY, YOU, are you fighting this battle or not?

'hereb', dagger or sword

depending on the length

bow and arrows

sword in the form of a sickle

catapult and stones

leather shield

pike or javelin

IN THE TIME OF KING SAUL, THE TRIBES OF ISRAEL WERE ASSEMBLED SEVERAL TIMES TO MAKE WAR ON A COMMON ENEMY. BUT EVEN THEN THE ARMY WAS NOT VERY LARGE. THE MEN GATHERED, DRESSED TO GO TO WORK IN THE FIELDS (A SHORT TUNIC), WITH THEIR ARMS (**SWORDS AND CATAPULTS**). **HELMETS AND ARMOR** WERE RARE BECAUSE THEY WERE TOO EXPENSIVE. BATTLES IN THE OPEN COUNTRY WERE OFTEN DISASTERS, BUT THE ACTIONS CARRIED OUT BY SMALL **COMMANDO GROUPS** HAD MORE SUCCESS, AS DID **TRAPS** AND **AMBUSHES**.

THE SPREAD OF CAVALRY

KING DAVID FORMED UNITS OF MERCENARIES. TO PRESERVE DAVID'S CONQUESTS, HIS SON SOLOMON CREATED LARGE DETACHMENTS OF WAR CHARIOTS AND ESTABLISHED FORTIFIED CITIES IN STRATEGIC PLACES, WHERE HE INSTALLED TROOPS.

WAR REPORT

SENNACHERIB, THE KING OF THE ASSYRIANS, CAMPED UNDER THE WALLS OF **LACHISH** AND SENT A MESSANGER TO RECEIVE THE SURRENDER OF THE CITY. THE DISCUSSIONS GOT NOWHERE AND A SIEGE OF THE CITY BEGAN. THE KING BROUGHT UP EARTH TO BUILD LONG RAMPS WHICH WOULD GIVE ACCESS TO THE WALLS. MEN WEARING WOODEN ARMOUR TO PROTECT THEM BATTERED THE WALLS WITH **RAMS** WHICH HAD IRON HEADS. THOSE UNDER SIEGE THREW **TORCHES** AND **STONES** AND FIRED **FLAMING ARROWS**. HOWEVER, THE ATTACKERS CLIMBED THE WALLS AND PENETRATED THE CITY THROUGH BREACHES MADE IN THE WALLS BY THE RAMS. **THE CITY FELL**.

701 BC. SIEGE OF LACHISH (A CITY FORTIFIED BY REHOBOAM) AFTER A BAS-RELIEF FOUND IN NINEVEH.

THE CONSEQUENCES OF WAR

NO HOPE FOR THE CONQUERED. THE CITIES WERE PLUNDERED, THEN **RAZED TO THE GROUND**. MEN, WOMEN AND CHILDREN WERE MASSACRED. SOMETIMES THE CONQUERED WERE REDUCED TO **SLAVERY** OR HAD TO **PAY HEAVY TRIBUTE**. THE ASSYRIANS AND BABYLONIANS PRACTISED **MASS DEPORTATIONS** OF CONQUERED PEOPLES.

THE MAN UPSTAIRS IS A CONSULTANT

THE MAN NEXT DOOR ON THE RIGHT IS A LAWYER

AND THE ONE ON THE LEFT IS A MAGISTRATE. ALL IMPORTANT AND POWERFUL PEOPLE

I FEEL SO SMALL AND CRUSHED!

POWERFUL AND DANGEROUS NEIGHBORS

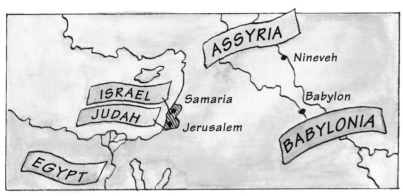

FROM 922 BC, THE TERRITORY OF ISRAEL WAS DIVIDED INTO **TWO KINGDOMS: ISRAEL**, WHOSE CAPITAL WAS FROM NOW ON TO BE **SAMARIA**, AND **JUDAH**, WITH **JERUSALEM** AS ITS CAPITAL. BORDERING ITS TERRITORY WERE
EGYPT TO THE SOUTH-WEST,
  ASSYRIA TO THE NORTH-EAST,
  AND **BABYLON** TO THE EAST.
THIS SITUATION HARDLY BROUGHT PEACE AND TRANQUILLITY.

THE ASSYRIANS, A PEOPLE OF FEROCIOUS WARRIORS

THE ASSYRIANS WERE GREAT EXPERTS AT WAR. THEIR LAND WAS NOT FERTILE, SO THEY WERE OBLIGED TO ATTACK THEIR NEIGHBORS TO SURVIVE.

ALL MALES HAD TO SERVE IN THE ARMY.

THE ARMY WAS VERY WELL ORGANIZED.

MILITARY ENGINEERS HAD GOT SIEGES TO A FINE ART.

Jewish prisoners prostrate themselves before Sennacherib and beg for mercy

THERE WAS NO HOPE FOR MOST OF THE CONQUERED: THOSE WHO WERE NOT KILLED WERE FORCIBLY DEPORTED AND THE REMAINING POPULATION HAD TO PAY HEAVY TRIBUTE. THIS WAS THE FATE OF THE **KINGDOM OF ISRAEL**, WHICH WAS INVADED, DESTROYED AND STRIPPED OF ITS INHABITANTS BEFORE DISAPPEARING FOR EVER FROM HISTORY IN 722 BC.

Jehu, king of Israel, prostrates himself before Shalmanezer III Obelisk from Nimrod

92 ONLY A CENTURY LATER, THE ASSYRIAN EMPIRE, WEAKENED BY A SERIES OF REVOLTS, WAS ANNIHILATED BY SIMULTANEOUS ATTACKS FROM NORTH AND SOUTH, WHERE **BABYLON** WAS RESUMING ITS POLICY OF EXPANSION.

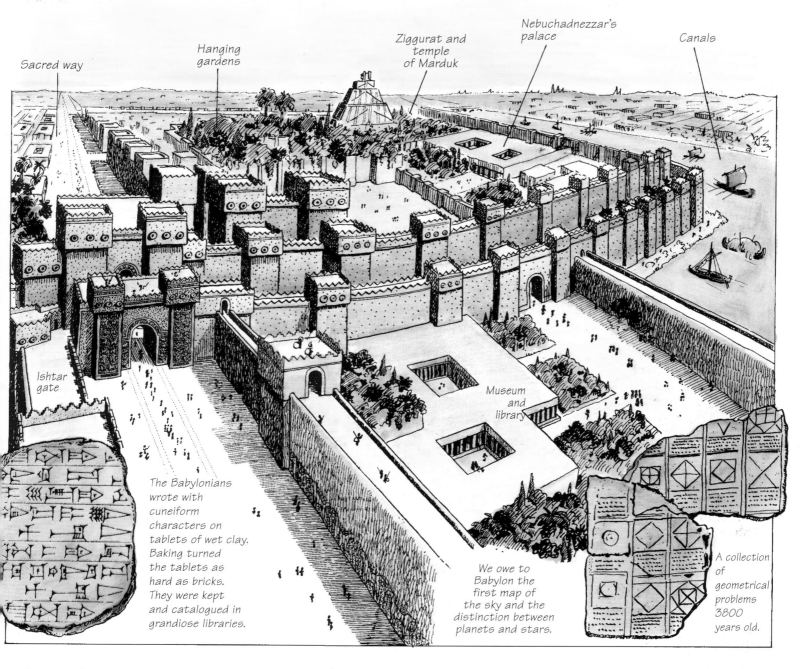

Sacred way

Hanging gardens

Ziggurat and temple of Marduk

Nebuchadnezzar's palace

Canals

Ishtar gate

Museum and library

The Babylonians wrote with cuneiform characters on tablets of wet clay. Baking turned the tablets as hard as bricks. They were kept and catalogued in grandiose libraries.

We owe to Babylon the first map of the sky and the distinction between planets and stars.

A collection of geometrical problems 3800 years old.

BABYLON AND THE KINGDOM OF JUDAH

DURING THE WARS OF EXPANSION WAGED BY THE BABYLONIAN KINGS, THE LITTLE **KINGDOM OF JUDAH** WAS SWEPT AWAY. IT LOST ITS INDEPENDENCE AND HAD TO PAY HEAVY TRIBUTE TO ITS CONQUERORS. AFTER TWO UNSUCCESSFUL REVOLTS, JERUSALEM AND THE TEMPLE WERE DESTROYED AND A LARGE PART OF THE POPULATION WAS DEPORTED (587 BC). IT SEEMED TO BE ALL OVER, THE PEOPLE OF ISRAEL CROSSED OFF THE MAP! HOWEVER . . .

THE COLLAPSE OF THE BABYLONIAN EMPIRE

TO THE EAST, THE **PERSIAN** EMPIRE, RULED BY KING **CYRUS**, WAS EXPANDING. AFTER VARIOUS CONQUESTS, IN 539 BC THE PERSIAN ARMY CAPTURED BABYLON, WEAKENED BY INTERNAL DISSENSIONS. THE CITY WHICH HAD SEEMED INVINCIBLE WAS INTEGRATED INTO THE PERSIAN EMPIRE. THANKS TO THE TOLERANT POLICY OF THE NEW SOVEREIGN, THE EXILES COULD RETURN HOME. AFTER FIFTY YEARS OF EXILE, THE JEWS, WHO REMEMBERED THEIR PAST, SET OUT FOR THEIR HOMELAND.

THE UNIVERSE SEEN BY...

ALL THE ANCIENT PEOPLES HAD THEIR OWN VIEW OF THE EARTH

...THE HEBREWS

IN ISRAEL, REFLECTION ON THE UNIVERSE DEVELOPED IN CONTACT WITH AND IN HOSTILE OPPOSITION TO BABYLONIAN THOUGHT, PARTICULARLY DURING THE EXILE. THE EARTH WAS THOUGHT OF AS A PLATFORM SURROUNDED BY OCEANS. IT RESTED ON PILLARS SUNK IN THE DEEP. THE FIRMAMENT FORMED A VAULT FROM WHICH THE STARS WERE SUSPENDED. THE VAULT KEEPING OUT THE WATERS ABOVE WAS FULL OF HOLES THROUGH WHICH THE RAIN CAME.

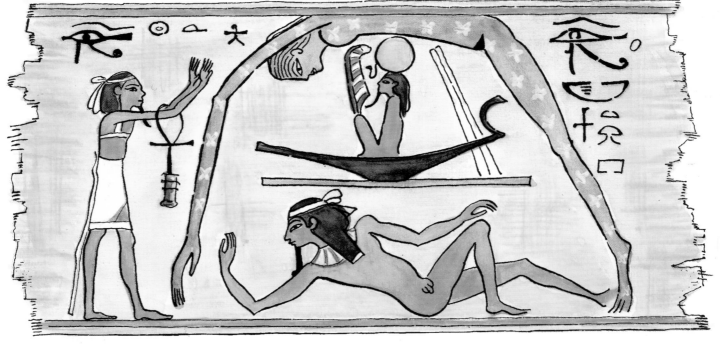

THE EGYPTIANS

SHU, GOD OF AIR AND LIGHT, SEPARATES NUT, GODDESS OF HEAVEN, FROM GEB, GOD OF THE EARTH. DURING THE DAY, THE SUN GOD RA SAILS IN HIS BOAT BETWEEN HEAVEN AND EARTH. AT NIGHT HE RESTS IN NUT'S BODY, TO BE BORN AGAIN EVERY MORNING.

94

THE NORDIC PEOPLES IMAGINED THE UNIVERSE AS A GIANT TREE IN THE MIDDLE OF A ROUND DISC PUT IN THE MIDDLE OF THE OCEAN. THE TREE HAS THREE ROOTS WHICH PENETRATE INTO THREE REALMS: THAT OF THE HUMAN RACE, THAT OF THE GIANTS OF OLD AND THAT OF THE DEAD. THE COURSE OF THE SUN IS REPRESENTED IN THE DAY BY A CHARIOT AND IN THE NIGHT BY A BOAT WHICH CROSSES THE UNDERGROUND WORLD.

THE INDIANS

IN INDIA, A TRIBE BELIEVED THAT THE EARTH WAS SUPPORTED BY ELEPHANTS AND THAT THEIR MOVEMENTS PRODUCED EARTHQUAKES.

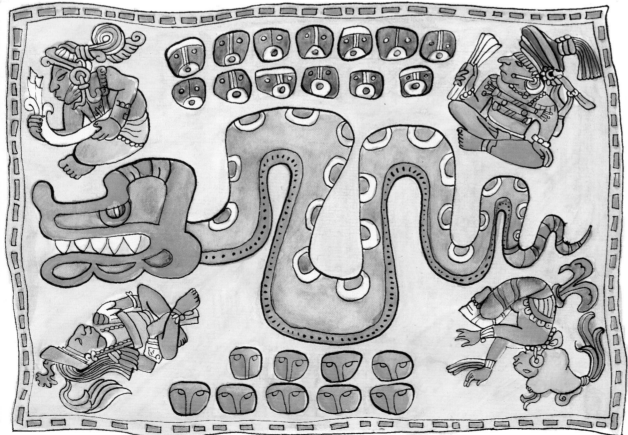

THE MAYAS

ACCORDING TO THE MAYAS, THE EARTH RESTS ON AN ENORMOUS SERPENT WHICH SWIMS ON THE OCEAN. NINE INFERNAL SPHERES UNDER THE EARTH ARE GUIDED BY NINE GODS (THE BOLANTI KU); ABOVE THE EARTH, THIRTEEN CELESTIAL SPHERES ARE GOVERNED BY THE OXLAHUNTI KU GODS. AT THE FOUR CORNERS OF THE EARTH ARE THE FOUR BACAB, GODS WHOSE TASK IS TO SUPPORT THE HEAVEN.

LISTEN! ONCE THE GREEKS INVADED THE NEAR EAST ...

THE JEWS BEGAN TO SPEAK LIKE THE GREEKS, DRESS LIKE THEM, THINK LIKE THEM ...

INCREDIBLE!

I'M GOING OUT FOR A MOMENT! CIAO!

OOPS!

THE SPREAD OF GREEK CULTURE

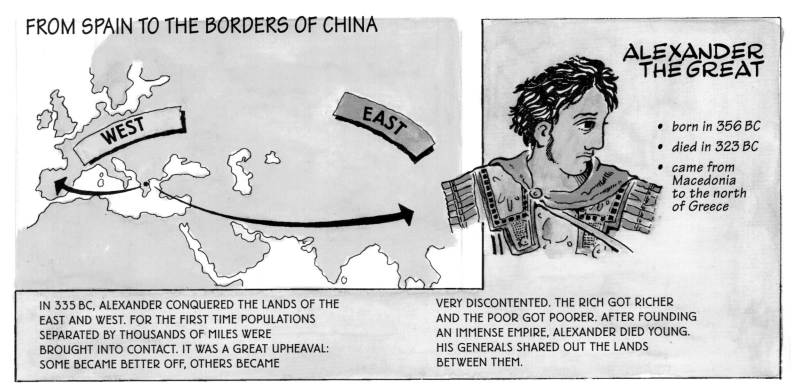

FROM SPAIN TO THE BORDERS OF CHINA

WEST

EAST

ALEXANDER THE GREAT

- born in 356 BC
- died in 323 BC
- came from Macedonia to the north of Greece

IN 335 BC, ALEXANDER CONQUERED THE LANDS OF THE EAST AND WEST. FOR THE FIRST TIME POPULATIONS SEPARATED BY THOUSANDS OF MILES WERE BROUGHT INTO CONTACT. IT WAS A GREAT UPHEAVAL: SOME BECAME BETTER OFF, OTHERS BECAME VERY DISCONTENTED. THE RICH GOT RICHER AND THE POOR GOT POORER. AFTER FOUNDING AN IMMENSE EMPIRE, ALEXANDER DIED YOUNG. HIS GENERALS SHARED OUT THE LANDS BETWEEN THEM.

CONSEQUENCE: THERE WAS A SPREAD ALL OVER THE WORLD OF ...

RELIGION

LIFE STYLE

DEAR FELLOW PHILOSOPHERS

LANGUAGE

ART

ΕΙΣ ΧΑλΟΥ ηΧΕΙΣ

THOUGHT

IT WAS NO NOVELTY
FOR ISRAEL
TO BE INVADED
BY FOREIGN
POWERS

PTUM PTUM PTUM PTUM PTUM PTUM PTUM PTUM

ASSYRIANS — BABYLONIANS — EGYPTIANS — PERSIANS — MACEDONIANS — ROMANS

BUT THIS TIME ...

THE INTRODUCTION OF GREEK CIVILIZATION PROVOKED LIVELY OPPOSITION FROM SOME PEOPLE WHILE OTHERS PASSIONATELY SUPPORTED IT.

Hey, Simon, how are things?

Shalom, Azariah! I hardly recognized you dressed like that!

I love Greek fashion. Indeed, I'm quite fond of going to the gymnasium from time to time.

What am I hearing? I hate all that! All this culture of the body and going about naked. Horrible! This imitating Greeks in everything is a disaster. It will cost us dear.

Don't exaggerate! Greek culture is at any rate bringing us a breath of fresh air. It's more open – international, even.

Quiet, you don't know what you're saying. If we don't remain faithful to the tradition, the invaders will swallow us up, us, our lands and our children.

You can be modern and remain faithful to your traditions.

No, no! If we adapt to the new civilization our country will never be free.

You're too pessimistic! Think of the advantages of a common language for business and foreign contacts. It's tremendous.

Bah! It may be useful for fortunate businessmen like you, but the others, the less fortunate ones, still go hungry. And don't forget that we've all lost our **freedom**, rich and poor, and seen our Temple desecrated. Life is nothing but suffering.

NEVERTHELESS, GREEK CULTURE SPREAD

IN THE OLDEST SYNAGOGUES, DESPITE THE BIBLICAL PROHIBITION, FRESCOES, FRIEZES AND MOSAICS HAVE BEEN FOUND WITH DECORATIONS DRAWN FROM THE VEGETABLE AND ANIMAL WORLD, ALONG WITH MYTHICAL SYMBOLS AND BOLD REPRESENTATIONS OF THE HUMAN BODY. RABBIS WERE TOLERANT ENOUGH TO AUTHORIZE DECORATION INSPIRED BY GREEK MYTHOLOGY.

Some figures from the frescoes of the synagogue of **Dura Europos** in Syria, built in 200 BC and destroyed in AD 256.

97

THE ROMANS IN PALESTINE

A MUCH SOUGHT-AFTER LAND

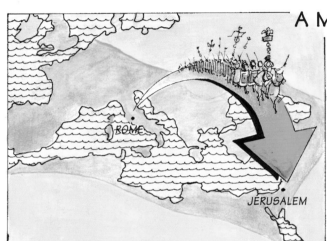

IN THE COURSE OF THE MANY WARS WHICH THEY WAGED TO EXPAND THEIR TERRITORY, THE ROMANS OCCUPIED PALESTINE AROUND 60 BC.

OVER LITTLE MORE THAN 500 YEARS ALL THESE PEOPLES – EXCEPT FOR VERY SHORT PERIODS – SUCCEEDED IN DOMINATING THIS VALUABLE **CORRIDOR** THROUGH WHICH SEA AND LAND TRAFFIC PASSED BETWEEN **WEST** AND **EAST**.

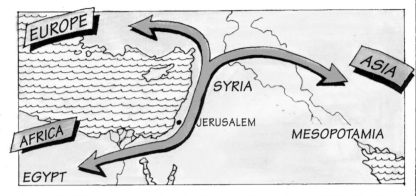

PALESTINE WAS THE HOMELAND OF THE JEWS IN ANCIENT TIMES. TODAY THE LAND IS DIVIDED BETWEEN THE STATE OF ISRAEL AND THE AUTONOMOUS PALESTINIAN TERRITORIES. IT IS SLIGHTLY SMALLER THAN BELGIUM, BUT ITS POSITION MAKES IT VERY INTERESTING TO THE **GREAT POWERS.**

A NEW PROVINCE

AFTER THE LAST CONQUEST, JUDAEA, IN THE SOUTH OF PALESTINE, BECAME A SECONDARY PROVINCE OF THE ROMAN EMPIRE, UNDER THE AUTHORITY OF:

THE EMPEROR

THE GOVERNOR

3000 soldiers and 500 extra soldiers in Jerusalem during the festivals

THE SANHEDRIN

The supreme Jewish council for religious and internal affairs. 70 representatives of the upper classes and the High priest.

THE ROYAL HOUSE OF JUDAEA

Herod and his descendants, with mercenary militia and foreigners

ON THE JEWISH SIDE

UNDER THE ROMAN OCCUPATION THE JEWS BENEFITED FROM A DEGREE OF AUTONOMY. BUT THE EMPEROR CULT, THE DEMANDS OF THE SOLDIERS AND THE EVER RISING TAXES SOON MADE THINGS UNBEARABLE FOR THE POPULATION.

HEAR, ISRAEL, THE LORD IS OUR GOD, THE LORD IS **ONE!**

Look, we're bringing you peace.

But in that case why are there so many soldiers everywhere?

Don't complain! It's to keep the peace.

OK, but the slightest gesture is enough to put one in prison or on the cross.

Keep calm and everything will get better: safe roads, circuses and theatres, the Temple rebuilt and even exemptions from military service, since you are so strict over your Sabbath.

Certainly! And it will all be paid for with our money. Not to mention all the wealth that goes to Rome. The taxes are crushing, the people can't take any more. Soon there'll be trouble.

THERE WERE NUMEROUS REVOLTS AGAINST THE ROMANS, WHICH WERE PUT DOWN WITH GREAT FORCE.

THE GREAT REVOLTS

THE PEOPLE WERE IN A DESPERATE SITUATION. THE PEASANTS GOT INTO DEBT AND THEN LOST THEIR LANDS. THERE WERE MORE AND MORE POOR PEOPLE IN TOWNS.

ARMED GROUPS FORMED, AS DID RELIGIOUS COMMUNITIES WHICH WERE COMPLETELY CUT OFF FROM THE LIFE OF THE COUNTRY. DISPUTES BETWEEN HEROD'S HEIRS LED TO THE DISMEMBERMENT OF THE STATE. THE GOVERNOR IMPOSED AN INCREASINGLY STRICT POLICY UNTIL **THE FIRST GREAT REVOLT** BROKE OUT IN AD 66.

ALL PALESTINE REBELLED. THE JEWS HAD SOME SUCCESSES BUT ROME RAPIDLY ASSEMBLED 4 LEGIONS (ABOUT 24,000 MEN).

THE REGIONS WON IN THE NORTH (GALILEE), JUDAEA RESISTED.

AD 70. THE STRONGHOLDS OF JERUSALEM FELL AND THE TEMPLE WAS DESTROYED, NEVER TO BE REBUILT.

MORE THAN A MILLION DEAD AND 100,000 PRISONERS, SOME OF WHOM WERE SENT TO ROME. A LEGION WAS INSTALLED IN JERUSALEM.

IN AD 131, A **SECOND GREAT REBELLION** BROKE OUT.

AFTER FOUR YEARS RESISTANCE, EVEN JERUSALEM WAS RECAPTURED. THE CITY WAS REBUILT AS A PAGAN CITY. JEWS WERE NO LONGER ALLOWED IN.

SUBSEQUENTLY, JEWS COULD ENTER THE HOLY CITY, BUT ONLY TO LAMENT THE DESTRUCTION OF THE TEMPLE NEAR THE **WAILING WALL.**

NOW I'M GOING TO HAVE A TRIP ROUND TOWN TO FULFIL MYSELF

GOING ROUND TOWN I CAN ALREADY BREATHE IN THE SCENT OF INDEPENDENCE, OF BEING GROWN-UP

WRooooM

WELL, PERHAPS I SHOULD START WITH A TRIP IN THE COUNTRY!

THE INHABITANTS of PALESTINE

A STREET IN JERUSALEM 2000 YEARS AGO

THE SEDAN CHAIR IS CARRYING A NOBLE LADY. **NOBLE FAMILIES** WERE OFTEN VERY RICH. THEY HAD SERVANTS, SLAVES AND BODYGUARDS (USUALLY FOREIGNERS). THEY OWNED LANDS, PALACES AND JEWELS AND LIVED A LIFE OF LUXURY AND PLEASURE.

GOING UP TO THE TEMPLE...

THE MOST IMPORTANT **PRIESTS** IN JERUSALEM WERE RICH. THE GARMENTS THEY WORE AT GREAT CEREMONIES WERE VERY EXPENSIVE. ONE TUNIC COST THE EQUIVALENT OF 10,000 DAYS' PAY, THIRTY YEARS' WORK.

Move over!

MAKE WAY!

Happily, my parents PAID FOR IT!

TRADERS AND PEASANTS

COMMERCE WITH DISTANT COUNTRIES WAS IN THE HANDS OF **GREAT MERCHANTS** WHO HAD THE MONEY NECESSARY FOR INVESTMENT, BUYING, TRANSPORTING AND STORING MERCHANDISE.

SMALL TRADERS SOLD LOCAL PRODUCE WHICH THEY TOOK FROM ONE VILLAGE TO ANOTHER.

PALESTINE IS A RATHER DRY REGION WITHOUT WATER, BUT MOST OF THE INHABITANTS WERE ENGAGED IN AGRICULTURE.

Where have you got to with the olive gathering?

It's almost finished.

THERE WERE NOT MANY **GREAT LANDOWNERS.** THEY RAN THEIR ESTATES, NEGOTIATED WITH MERCHANTS AND HAD A CERTAIN NUMBER OF ADMINISTRATORS WHO IN TURN RECRUITED AND SUPERVISED LABORERS.

MOST OF THE POPULATION WERE **PEASANTS.** THEY USUALLY HAD SUFFICIENT LAND TO PRODUCE ENOUGH TO SUPPORT A FAMILY. THE SURPLUS WAS EXCHANGED FOR OTHER INDISPENSABLE GOODS.

IN A VILLAGE 2000 YEARS AGO

SOLDIERS OF THE ROMAN ARMY AND **FOREIGN MERCENARIES** IN THE SERVICE OF THE GREAT LORDS WENT ALL OVER THE COUNTRY. NATURALLY THE POPULATION MISTRUSTED THEM AND AVOIDED CONTACT WITH THEM. THE SAMARITANS WERE THOROUGHLY DETESTED. JEWS AND **SAMARITANS** HAD HATED EACH OTHER FOR CENTURIES.

THE **PUBLICANS** COLLECTED TAXES FOR THE ROMANS. THEY WERE DESPISED BECAUSE THEY COLLABORATED WITH THE OCCUPYING FORCES BUT ALSO BECAUSE THEY DEMANDED MORE THAN THEY WERE DUE AND POCKETED THE DIFFERENCE.

THESE PEOPLE ARE **VERY POOR**. THEY ARE HIRED FOR THE DAY (FROM DAWN TO SUNSET) AND PAID A DENARIUS PLUS THE MID-DAY MEAL. A DENARIUS BUYS 6 KILOS OF BREAD.

THOSE WITH **CONTAGIOUS DISEASES** ARE KEPT AWAY TO PROTECT EVERYONE'S HEALTH. THEY LOSE THEIR CIVIL RIGHTS. THEY OFTEN LIVE IN SMALL GROUPS, HELPED AND FED BY THEIR FAMILIES.

A SICK PERSON ON THE POINT OF BEING HEALED HAS TO BE CHECKED BY A PRIEST. IF THE HEALING IS CONFIRMED, HE IS REINTEGRATED INTO THE TOWN.

IN EVERY CITY, TOWN AND VILLAGE, ESPECIALLY JERUSALEM, THERE ARE PEOPLE WHO HAVE NO WORK. THESE ARE OFTEN **THE CRIPPLED AND THE BLIND**, WHO ARE FORCED TO BEG FOR A LIVING. THE LAW OF ISRAEL CONSTANTLY EXHORTS PEOPLE NOT TO NEGLECT **THE POOR, THE WIDOWS** AND **THE ORPHANS**.

TRAVELLERS AND **FOREIGN MERCHANTS** ARE GIVEN A WARM WELCOME AND ARE PROTECTED, BUT THEY DO NOT HAVE THE RIGHT TO ENTER THE TEMPLE OF JERUSALEM. ONLY THOSE WHO HAVE LIVED IN THE COUNTRY FOR A LONG TIME AND ACCEPT THE JEWISH RELIGION AND ITS RULES CAN BECOME MEMBERS OF THE JEWISH PEOPLE.

... IN THE TIME OF JESUS

JERUSALEM ... IN THE TIME OF JESUS

AFTER ITS DESTRUCTION BY THE BABYLONIAN ARMY IN 587 BC, JERUSALEM WAS REBUILT VERY SLOWLY BY THE RETURNING EXILES AND THEIR DESCENDANTS. THE REAL REBUILDING WAS THE WORK OF **HEROD**. DRAWING HIS INSPIRATION FROM ROMAN ARCHITECTURAL MODELS, HE BUILT THE **ROYAL PALACE, ANTONIA FORTRESS**, THE **TEMPLE** AND THE **STRONG WALLS**. BY THE TIME OF JESUS, THE HOLY CITY HAD REGAINED ALL ITS ANCIENT SPLENDOR. THOSE GOING UP TOWARDS THE TEMPLE COULD SEE THOUSANDS OF MEN AT WORK.

Garden gate

To Jaffa

Herod's palace

Hasmonaean palace

Essene gate

Valley of Gehenna

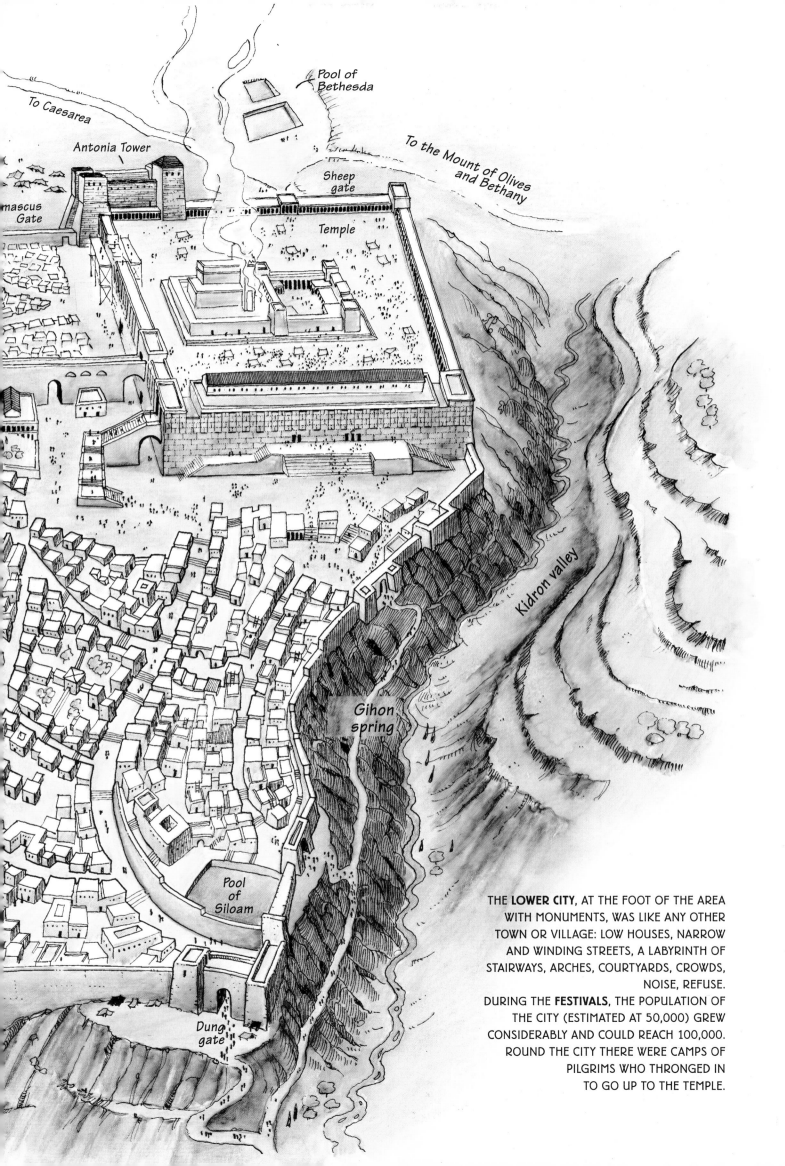

To Caesarea

Antonia Tower

mascus Gate

Pool of Bethesda

To the Mount of Olives and Bethany

Sheep gate

Temple

Kidron valley

Gihon spring

Pool of Siloam

Dung gate

THE **LOWER CITY**, AT THE FOOT OF THE AREA WITH MONUMENTS, WAS LIKE ANY OTHER TOWN OR VILLAGE: LOW HOUSES, NARROW AND WINDING STREETS, A LABYRINTH OF STAIRWAYS, ARCHES, COURTYARDS, CROWDS, NOISE, REFUSE. DURING THE **FESTIVALS**, THE POPULATION OF THE CITY (ESTIMATED AT 50,000) GREW CONSIDERABLY AND COULD REACH 100,000. ROUND THE CITY THERE WERE CAMPS OF PILGRIMS WHO THRONGED IN TO GO UP TO THE TEMPLE.

HERE'S A QUITE ORDINARY CUP ...

SLLOK!

WHICH 2000 YEARS FROM NOW WILL BE A VERY INTERESTING ARCHAEOLOGICAL RELIC!

THE ADVENTURE OF THE PAST

HERE ARE OUR EXCAVATIONS AT TELL ES-SULTAN, ANCIENT JERICHO!

IN THE NEAR EAST THERE ARE MANY HILLS, CALLED **'TELL'** IN ARABIC. THEY CONTAIN THE REMAINS OF ANCIENT CITIES, AND BY DIGGING DEEP IT IS POSSIBLE TO RECOVER THE REMAINS OF SEVERAL CITIES BUILT ONE ON TOP OF ANOTHER. THE DEEPEST ARE THE EARLIEST.

JERICHO, THE MOST ANCIENT CITY IN THE WORLD!

EXCAVATING AT TELL EL-SULTAN, NEAR PRESENT-DAY JERICHO, THE ENGLISH ARCHAEOLOGIST KATHLEEN KENYON FOUND NO LESS THAN SEVENTEEN LEVELS. MORE THAN 60 FEET DOWN SHE FOUND DWELLINGS GOING BACK MORE THAN 10,000 YEARS.

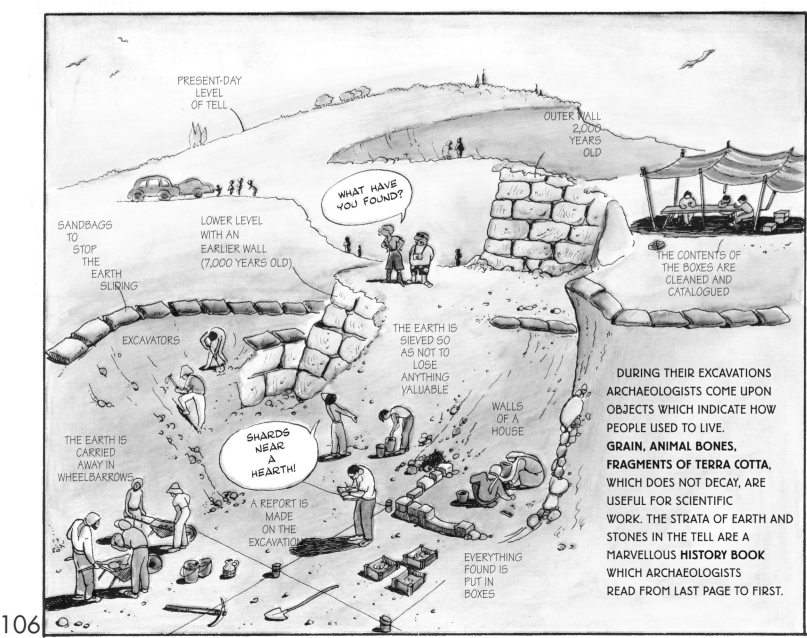

PRESENT-DAY LEVEL OF TELL

OUTER WALL 2,000 YEARS OLD

SANDBAGS TO STOP THE EARTH SLIDING

LOWER LEVEL WITH AN EARLIER WALL (7,000 YEARS OLD)

WHAT HAVE YOU FOUND?

THE CONTENTS OF THE BOXES ARE CLEANED AND CATALOGUED

EXCAVATORS

THE EARTH IS SIEVED SO AS NOT TO LOSE ANYTHING VALUABLE

WALLS OF A HOUSE

THE EARTH IS CARRIED AWAY IN WHEELBARROWS

SHARDS NEAR A HEARTH!

A REPORT IS MADE ON THE EXCAVATION

EVERYTHING FOUND IS PUT IN BOXES

DURING THEIR EXCAVATIONS ARCHAEOLOGISTS COME UPON OBJECTS WHICH INDICATE HOW PEOPLE USED TO LIVE. **GRAIN, ANIMAL BONES, FRAGMENTS OF TERRA COTTA,** WHICH DOES NOT DECAY, ARE USEFUL FOR SCIENTIFIC WORK. THE STRATA OF EARTH AND STONES IN THE TELL ARE A MARVELLOUS **HISTORY BOOK** WHICH ARCHAEOLOGISTS READ FROM LAST PAGE TO FIRST.

MM ... FOOTPRINTS ...

... OF A MAN WITH BIG SHOES WALKING QUICKLY ...

PERHAPS SO AS NOT TO MISS HIS TRAIN, UNLESS HE IS UNEMPLOYED AND HIS WIFE CAN'T FEED THEIR CHILDREN ...

I'D MAKE A GOOD ARCHAEOLOGIST!

THE TRACES OF THE PAST: FOUR ARCHAEOLOGICAL ADVENTURES

ARCHAEOLOGY IS THE SCIENCE OF DISCOVERING TRACES OF PAST HISTORY BY INVESTIGATING LAND AND STUDYING ANCIENT OBJECTS. THERE HAVE BEEN MANY ARCHAEOLOGICAL EXPEDITIONS TO PALESTINE AND THE ANCIENT NEAR EAST, AND STILL ARE TODAY. SOMETIMES EVIDENCE OF THE BIBLICAL PAST HAS BEEN DISCOVERED. MORE OFTEN, THE OBJECTS FOUND ALLOW US TO KNOW MORE ABOUT HOW MEN, WOMEN AND CHILDREN LIVED IN THE AREAS WHERE JEWS WERE SETTLED OR IN NEIGHBORING REGIONS WHICH PLAYED A ROLE IN THEIR EXISTENCE. A NUMBER OF ILLUSTRATIONS IN THIS BOOK REPRESENTING SCENES OF EVERYDAY LIFE (DWELLING PLACES, OBJECTS, CLOTHING, CUSTOMS, ETC.) ARE INSPIRED BY ANCIENT OBJECTS NOW IN MUSEUMS ALL OVER THE WORLD.

THE SILOAM INSCRIPTION

IN 1856, E. ROBINSON EXPLORED A TUNNEL IN **JERUSALEM** WHICH STARTED FROM A SPRING IN THE KIDRON VALLEY OUTSIDE THE CITY, TURNED SOUTHWARDS AND ENDED AT THE **POOL OF SILOAM**. THE DISCOVERY WENT UNNOTICED UNTIL ONE DAY IN 1880 WHEN A BOY BATHING IN THE POOL SAW AN INSCRIPTION IN HEBREW IN A FAIRLY INCONSPICUOUS PLACE. THE INSCRIPTION TELLS HOW THE TWO GROUPS WHICH DUG THE TUNNEL, ONE FROM THE NORTH AND THE OTHER FROM THE SOUTH, SUCCEEDED IN MEETING UP AND HOW, THANKS TO THE SLOPE IN THE TUNNEL, THE WATER REACHED THE RESERVOIR (SEE THE ILLUSTRATION ON P.81). THE INSCRIPTION IS NOT DATED, BUT STUDY OF THE SCRIPT PUTS IT AT THE END OF THE

EIGHTH CENTURY BC. SO IT MUST BE CONTEMPORARY WITH THE REIGN OF **HEZEKIAH** (716-687 BC). THE BIBLE RECORDS THIS GIGANTIC WORK COMMISSIONED BY THE KING (II KINGS 20. 20). IN THIS CASE, THE INSCRIPTION FOUND AND THE BIBLICAL NARRATIVE AGREE.

COURTYARD

KITCHEN

RITUAL BATH

THE BURNT DOWN HOUSE

IN RECENT EXCAVATIONS THE REMAINS HAVE BEEN DISCOVERED AND OPENED UP OF A HOUSE FROM THE TIME OF **HEROD**, WHICH WAS BURNT DOWN BY THE ROMAN ARMY - ON THE ORDERS OF TITUS - DURING THE DESTRUCTION OF **JERUSALEM** IN AD 70. THIS IS THE BASEMENT OF A BUILDING WHICH WAS CERTAINLY LARGER. THE DIFFERENT ROOMS CONTAIN OBJECTS FOR MILLING, MEASURING AND COOKING.

THE BOAT FROM THE SEA OF GALILEE

IN 1985-6, BECAUSE OF A GREAT DROUGHT, IT WAS DECIDED TO PUMP WATER FROM THE **SEA OF GALILEE** TO THE ADJOINING COUNTRYSIDE. PARTS OF THE BOTTOM, USUALLY COVERED WITH WATER, BECAME DRY. TWO BOYS TURNED INTO AMATEUR ARCHAEOLOGISTS AND SET OUT IN SEARCH OF ANCIENT OBJECTS. ONE DAY, FORTUNE SMILED ON THEM: THEY STUMBLED ON A BOAT

ALMOST COMPLETELY COVERED IN SILT. GREAT EXCITEMENT! WAS IT ANCIENT OR MODERN? IN THE COUNTRIES AROUND THE MEDITERRANEAN, SMALL BOATS WERE MADE WITH DISTINCTIVE TECHNIQUES. REMOVING THE MUD WITH EXTREME CARE, EXPERTS DISCOVERED THE CHARACTERISTICS OF THE BOAT. IT WAS CERTAINLY VERY OLD – AT LEAST TWO THOUSAND YEARS OLD! THERE WAS GREAT ENTHUSIASM AND ANOTHER RACE AGAINST TIME WAS NEEDED TO PRESERVE THE PRECIOUS DISCOVERY. THE WATER LEVEL HAD TO BE RESTORED, AND DOZENS OF VOLUNTEERS WORKED AROUND THE BOAT TO FREE IT FROM THE MUD, PROTECT IT AND TRANSFER IT TO ITS DESTINATION, THE YGAL MUSEUM, A WHITE BUILDING WHICH TOWERS ABOVE THE SEA OF GALILEE.

Lamp found inside the boat

Clay cooking vessel found near the boat

MASADA

THE FORTRESS OF MASADA WAS BUILT BY **HEROD** NEAR THE **DEAD SEA** ON THE FLAT SUMMIT OF A MOUNTAIN PROTECTED ON ALL SIDES BY SHEER CLIFFS. IT WAS THE LAST BUILDING OF THIS ARCHITECT KING AND ALSO THE LAST REFUGE OF THE JEWISH REBELS IN THE JEWISH REVOLT AGAINST ROME. THEY RESISTED UNTIL AD 73. ON THE EVE OF THE ASSAULT BY THE ROMAN TROOPS, THEY DECIDED TO COMMIT MASS SUICIDE SO AS NOT TO FALL INTO THE HANDS OF THE ATTACKERS.

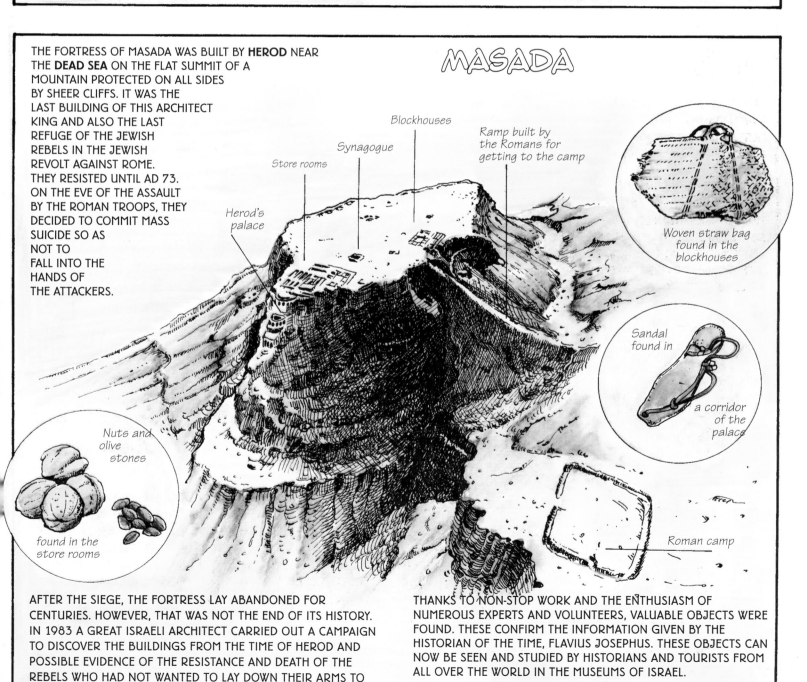

Store rooms

Synagogue

Blockhouses

Ramp built by the Romans for getting to the camp

Herod's palace

Woven straw bag found in the blockhouses

Sandal found in a corridor of the palace

Nuts and olive stones found in the store rooms

Roman camp

AFTER THE SIEGE, THE FORTRESS LAY ABANDONED FOR CENTURIES. HOWEVER, THAT WAS NOT THE END OF ITS HISTORY. IN 1983 A GREAT ISRAELI ARCHITECT CARRIED OUT A CAMPAIGN TO DISCOVER THE BUILDINGS FROM THE TIME OF HEROD AND POSSIBLE EVIDENCE OF THE RESISTANCE AND DEATH OF THE REBELS WHO HAD NOT WANTED TO LAY DOWN THEIR ARMS TO THE ROMAN ARMY.

THANKS TO NON-STOP WORK AND THE ENTHUSIASM OF NUMEROUS EXPERTS AND VOLUNTEERS, VALUABLE OBJECTS WERE FOUND. THESE CONFIRM THE INFORMATION GIVEN BY THE HISTORIAN OF THE TIME, FLAVIUS JOSEPHUS. THESE OBJECTS CAN NOW BE SEEN AND STUDIED BY HISTORIANS AND TOURISTS FROM ALL OVER THE WORLD IN THE MUSEUMS OF ISRAEL.

Claire Rollier Musatti has two great passions which she has succeeded in combining in her work: the Bible and children. She has taught in primary schools and for a long time has been a catechist in the Waldensian Church. She now lives and works in Milan as an educator.

Silvia Gastaldi Chiarenzi has been designing children's books since 1971. Her experience as a catechist with children in the Baptist Church has allowed her to make use of her knowledge both of young people, their psychology and their sense of humor, and her interest in archaeology. Like Claire Rollier Musatti, she lives and works in Milan.

Original Italian edition
Il popolo del Libro,
© Claudiana Editrice 1998
© Editrice ELLEDICI 1998

The French version on which this edition is based was published by:
Éditions du Signe, BP 94 – F67038 Strasbourg Cedex 2, France
© Éditions du Signe 1999

Idea by Silvia Gastaldi and Claire Musatti.

Drawings by Silvia Gastaldi

Cover by Silvia Gastaldi

Cartoons by Sandro Spanu

Watercolors by Elisa Corsani

English translation copyright © John Bowden 2000

This edition published 2001 by St. Anthony Messenger Press, 1615 Republic Street, Cincinnati, OH 45210, 1-800-488-0488, www.AmericanCatholic.org

ISBN (U.S.) 0-86716-468-9

All rights reserved.

Printed in Italy by PozzoGrosMonti, Torino

INDEX